The MAILBOX®

The Education Center®

5/11

P9-EDX-458

Everything Themes

grades PreK-K

Timesaving tools for important skills practice

- Theme practice pages
- Programmable cards
- Literacy and math practice
- Class book activities

- Quick crafts
- Fine-motor fun

Activities for 20 different themes!

Managing Editor: Kelly Robertson

Editorial Team: Becky S. Andrews, Diane Badden, Kimberley Bruck, Karen A. Brudnak, Pam Crane, Sarah Foreman, Pierce Foster, Ada Goren, Tazmen Hansen, Marsha Heim, Lori Z. Henry, Debra Liverman, Kitty Lowrance, Jennifer Nunn, Tina Petersen, Mark Rainey, Greg D. Rieves, Hope Rodgers, Donna K. Teal, Rachael Traylor, Sharon M. Tresino

www.themailbox.com

©2010 The Mailbox® Books
All rights reserved.
ISBN10 #1-56234-933-3 • ISBN13 #978-1-56234-933-2

Printed in the United States
10 9 8 7 6 5 4 3 2 1

HPS 211921

What's

theme-related pages

fun practice pages

Inside

programmable picture cards

quick crafts

Just Hatched

Materials: white construction paper copy of this page, crayons, scissors, glue, brad fastener

Directions: Color the baby dinosaur. Cut out the patterns and cut the egg apart. Glue the baby dinosaur to the bottom half of the egg as shown. Place the top half of the egg atop the bottom half, slightly overlapping the two pieces. Use the brad to attach the egg halves.

Lion's Hairdo

Materials: orange, yellow, and brown paper strips; paper plate; crayons; scissors; glue; unsharpened pencil

Directions: Color and cut out the lion's face. Glue the face in the center of the plate. Curl each paper strip by rolling it around the pencil. Then glue the curled strips around the rim of the plate to create the lion's mane.

Plus more ways to use the teaching tools!

class book activities

Space Sights!

If I took a trip in a spaceship, I might see

_____

by _____

Table of Contents

Apples

Note to the teacher: Read aloud the theme title. Then name each picture and invite youngsters to describe how it does or does not relate to apples. Have a child circle each picture that can be related to apples and cross out each picture that cannot. *Only the hanger does not relate to apples. Less obvious pictures that do relate to apples are the sun (needed to grow apples) and the lunch bag (may contain an apple).*

Apple Cards

See pages 172–174 for ways to use the cards.

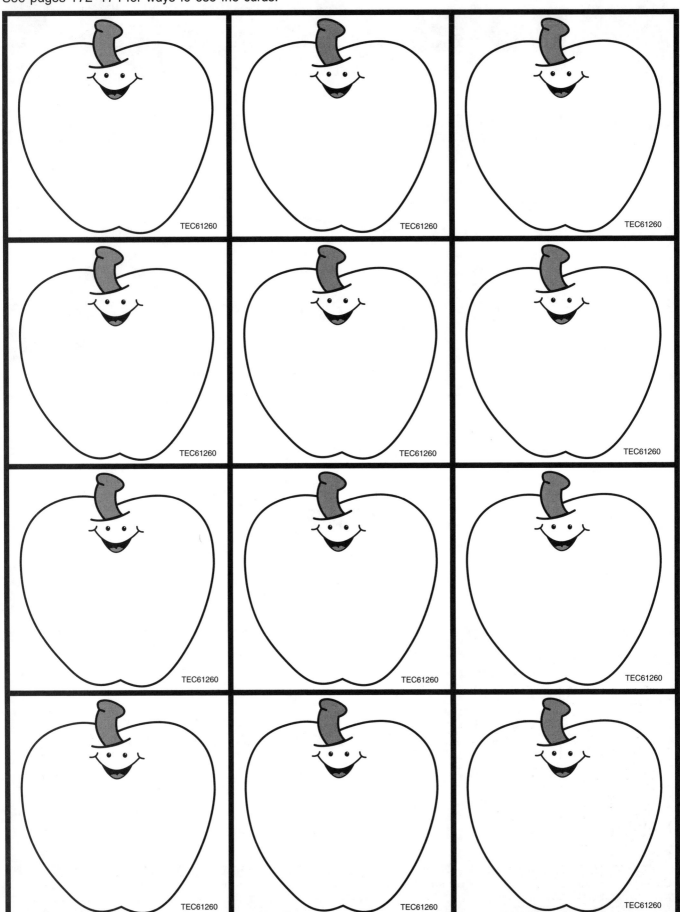

Everything Themes • ©The Mailbox® Books • TEC61260

My Apple Ideas

The very best apples are _____

_____ .

I like these apples best because _____

_____

_____ .

by _____

Listen and Do

Draw.

Note to the teacher: Provide oral directions, such as "Color the apple with a leaf and a stem green" or "Circle the apple slice with two seeds." Then specify what you would like the child to draw in the empty box by saying, for example, "Draw four apple seeds in the box."

Prizewinning Apples

Cut.

Glue.

1st

Name _____

10

Fresh From the Oven

✂ Cut.

🗴 Glue to match rhyming pictures.

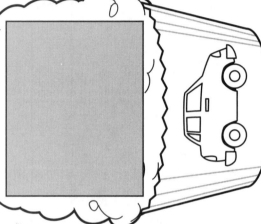

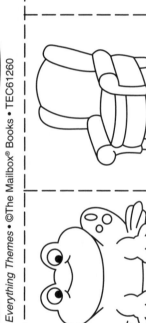

In the Orchard

Draw apples to match each number.

2 :

5 ⠿

4 ∷

3 ⠇

1 ⠒

Everything Themes • ©The Mailbox® Books • TEC61260

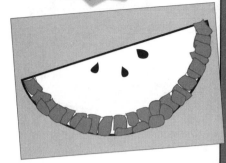

Apple Slice Art

Materials: 5" x 8" sheet of tagboard; construction paper scraps for apple skin (red, green, or yellow) and seeds (brown or black); glue; scissors

Directions: Cut out the apple slice pattern and glue the cutout to the tagboard. Tear the paper scraps for the apple skin into small pieces and glue them in the corresponding section of the cutout. Tear three seed shapes from the paper scraps. Glue each one on a different dot.

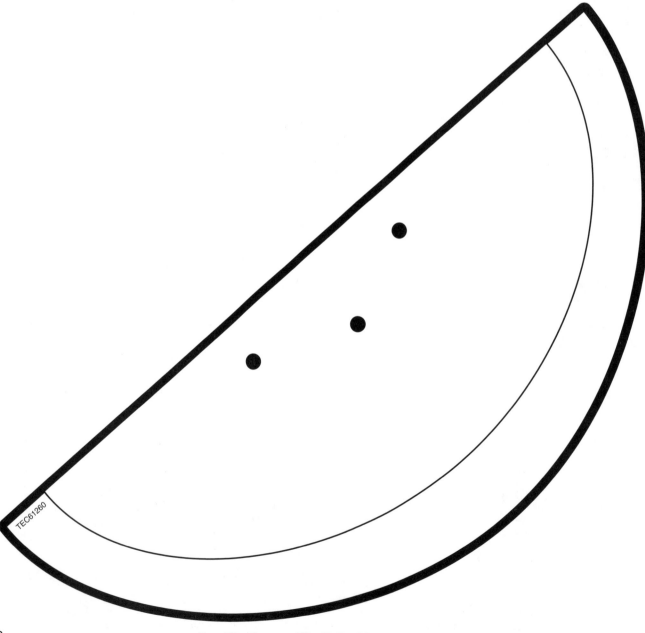

TEC61260

Beach

Note to the teacher: Read aloud the theme title. Then name each picture and invite youngsters to describe how it does or does not relate to the beach. Have a child circle each picture that can be related to the beach and cross out each picture that cannot. *The mittens do not relate to the beach. Less obvious pictures that do relate to the beach are the kite (often flown at the beach) and the flip-flops (may be worn at the beach).*

Seashell Cards

See pages 172–174 for ways to use the cards.

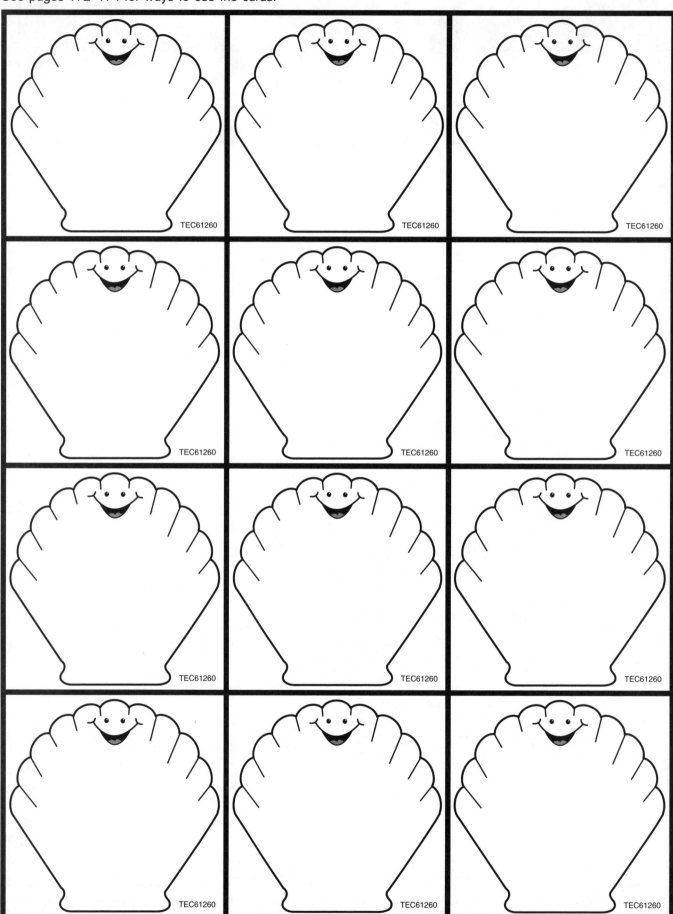

A Day at the Beach

At the beach, I like to

by ____________________

Everything Themes • ©The Mailbox® Books • TEC61260

Class Book Page: Have a child write or dictate a response to the prompt. Then have her illustrate her work. Publish the pages in a class book titled "Fun at the Beach."

Listen and Do

Draw.

Note to the teacher: Provide oral directions, such as "Color the striped beach towel" or "Circle the items that could be used to build a sand castle." Then specify what you would like the child to draw in the empty box by saying, for example, "Draw a creature you might see at the beach."

Pretty Shells

 Cut.

Glue.

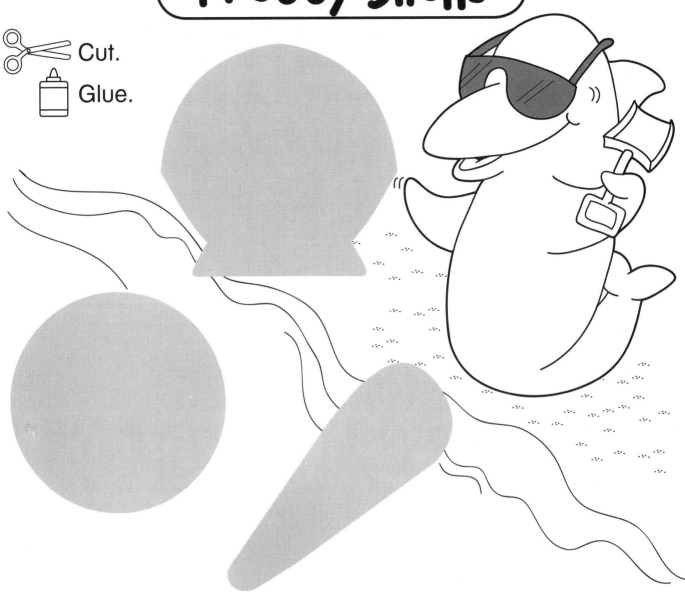

Everything Themes • ©The Mailbox® Books • TEC61260

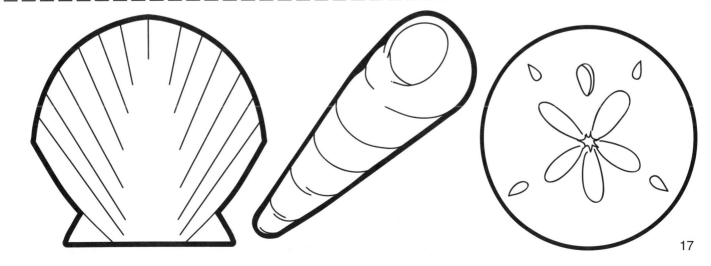

Collecting Shells

Color the shells with matching letter pairs.

T T   M R   K K

S L   D D   P F

B B   J J

Everything Themes • ©The Mailbox® Books • TEC61260

Name

One-to-one correspondence

Playing in the Sand

✂ Cut.

🧴 Glue to match one to one.

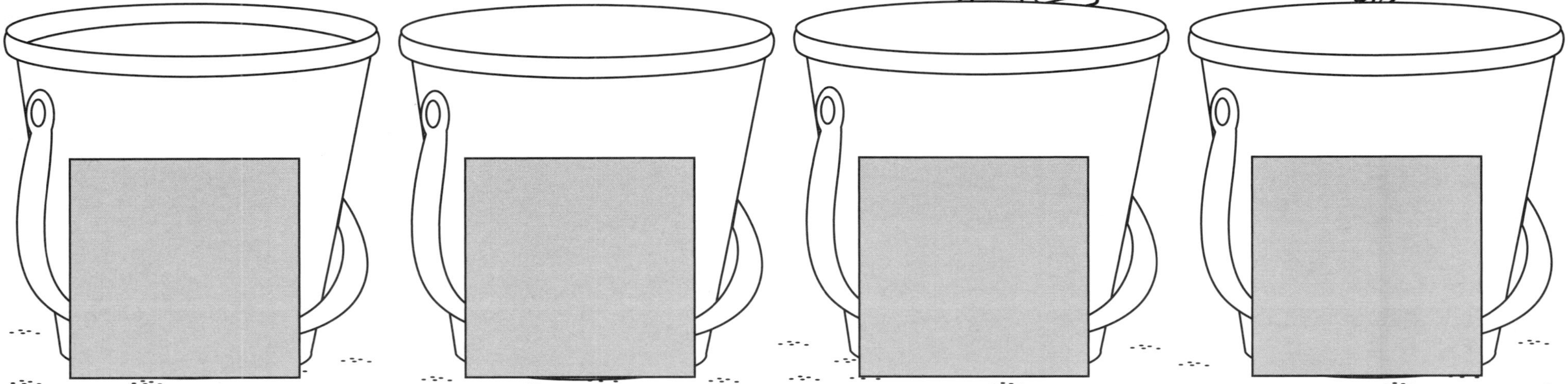

Everything Themes • ©The Mailbox® Books • TEC61260

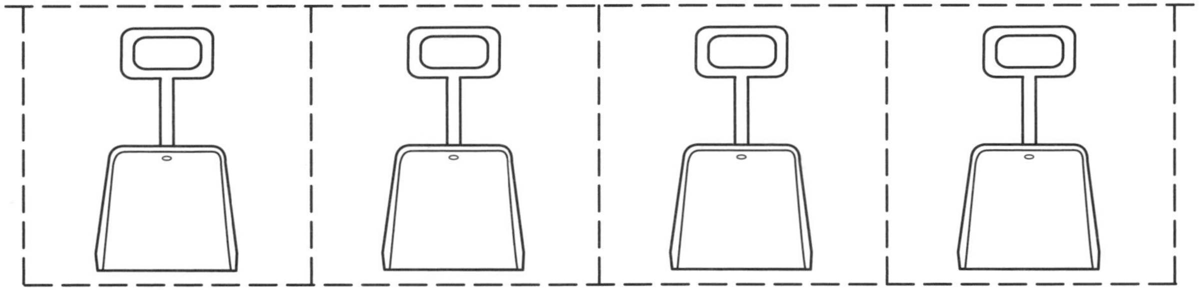

19

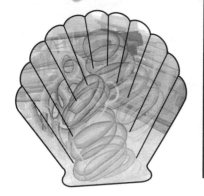

Quick Craft

Colorful Seashell

Materials: construction paper copy of this page, sidewalk chalk, hair spray

Directions: Rub various colors of sidewalk chalk on the seashell pattern; then blend the colors together with your fingers. Cut out the seashell and spray it lightly with hair spray to set the chalk.

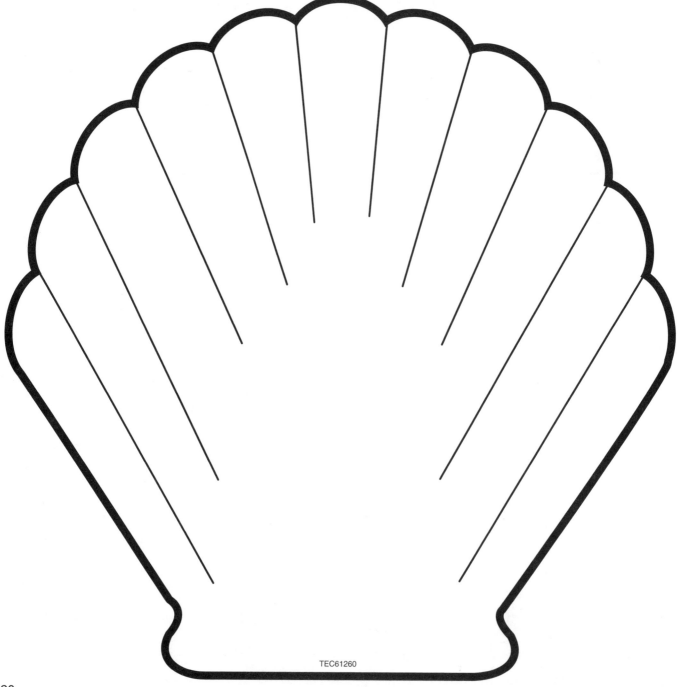

TEC61260

Everything Themes • ©The Mailbox® Books • TEC61260

Bears

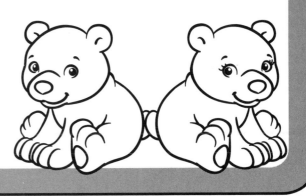

Note to the teacher: Read aloud the theme title. Then name each picture and invite youngsters to describe how it does or does not relate to bears. Have a child circle each picture that can be related to bears and cross out each picture that cannot. *The car and the pants do not relate to bears. Less obvious pictures that do relate to bears are the beehive (bears might get honey from one), the tree (bears can climb trees), and the fish (some bears eat fish).*

Teddy Bear Cards

See pages 172–174 for ways to use the cards.

TEC61260

A Great Bear

My favorite kind of bear is a _____

_____

because _____

_____

_____.

by _____

Listen and Do

Draw.

Note to the teacher: Provide oral directions, such as "Color the bear that is a stuffed toy" or "Circle the baby bear." Then specify what you would like the child to draw in the empty box by saying, for example, "Draw eight bear pawprints."

Time for Bed

Trace.

Name _____

Yummy Honey

Color the 3 rhyming pictures in each row.

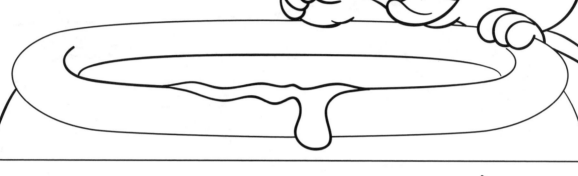

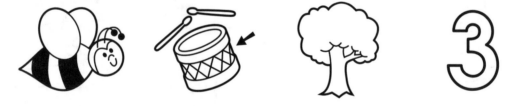

Teddy's Family

 Cut.

Glue to complete each pattern.

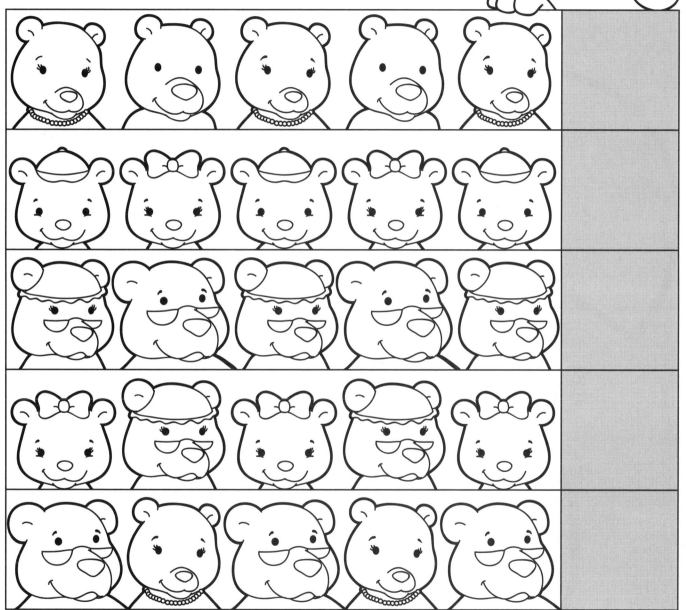

Everything Themes • ©The Mailbox® Books • TEC61260

Quick Craft

Big Brown Bear

Materials: paper plate, brown paper scraps, crayons, scissors, glue

Directions: Color and cut out the patterns. Tear the brown paper and glue the pieces to the paper plate. Then glue the patterns to the plate as shown. Draw two eyes to complete the bear's face.

TEC61260

Bugs

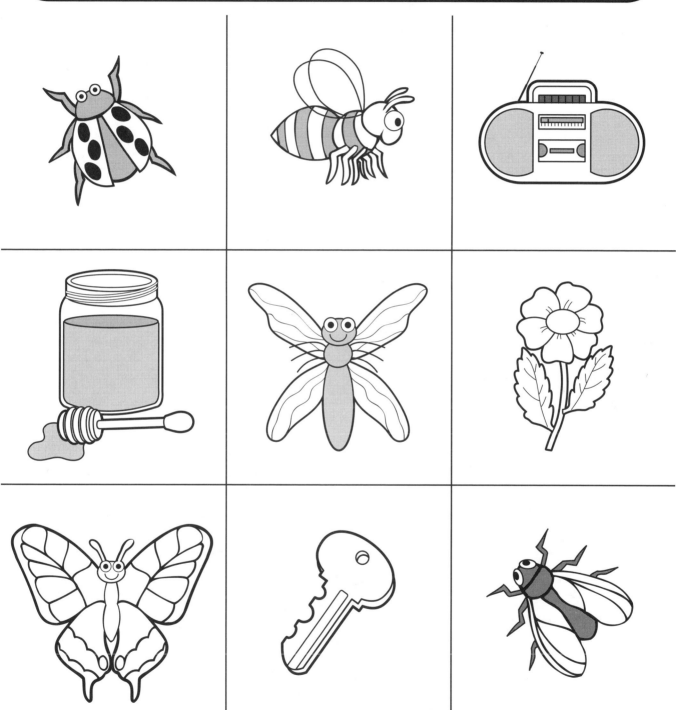

Note to the teacher: Read aloud the theme title. Then name each picture and invite youngsters to describe how it does or does not relate to bugs. Have a child circle each picture that can be related to bugs and cross out each picture that cannot. *The radio and the key do not relate to bugs. Less obvious pictures that do relate to bugs are the pot of honey (some bees make honey) and the flower (some bugs pollinate flowers).*

Beetle Cards
See pages 172–174 for ways to use the cards.

TEC61260

TEC61260

TEC61260

TEC61260

TEC61260

TEC61260

TEC61260

TEC61260

TEC61260

TEC61260

TEC61260

TEC61260

Everything Themes • ©The Mailbox® Books • TEC61260

Going Buggy!

If I could be any bug, I would be

_____

because _____

_____.

by _____

Class Book Page: Have a child write or dictate to complete the sentence. Then have her illustrate her work. Publish the pages in a class book titled "Becoming Bugs."

Listen and Do

Draw.

Note to the teacher: Provide oral directions, such as "Color a bug that is red with black spots" or "Circle a bug that lives in a hive." Then specify what you would like the child to draw in the empty box by saying, for example, "Draw six flowers."

Name _____

Flying Along

 Cut.

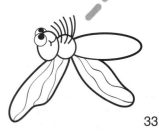

Everything Themes • ©The Mailbox® Books • TEC61260

33

Uppercase and lowercase letters

Buzzing Around

Color the 🐝 with matching letter pairs.

 Bf
 Ee
 Hh

 Jj
 Kl
 Mm

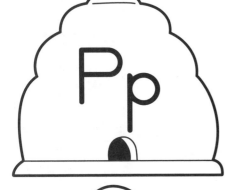 Pp
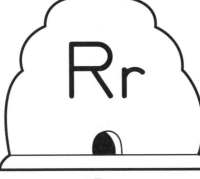 Rr
 Sc

 Uu
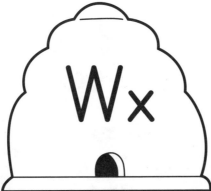 Wx
 Yy

Lots of Bugs

✂ Cut.

🧴 Glue to make a graph.

Types of Bugs

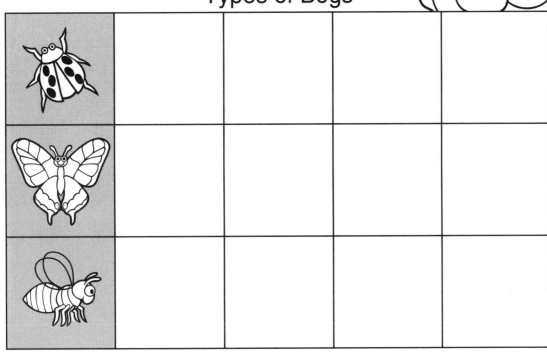

✏ Write how many.

 _____    _____    _____

🔍✏ Circle. Which has the most?

In the Ant Farm

Materials: 9" paper square, black ink pad, thin black marker, scissors, glue, crayons

Directions: Color the soil portion of the ant farm. Cut out the ant farm and glue it to the paper square. Then press your fingertip on an ink pad and make three consecutive fingerprints so they resemble an ant. Make several other ants in the same manner. Use the marker to add details to each ant.

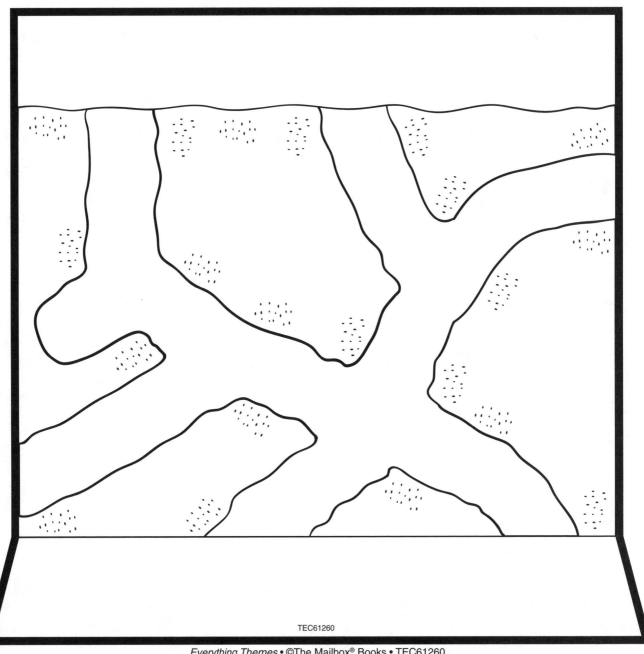

TEC61260

Circus

Note to the teacher: Read aloud the theme title. Then name each picture and invite youngsters to describe how it does or does not relate to a circus. Have a child circle each picture that can be related to a circus and cross out each picture that cannot. *The football does not relate to a circus. Less obvious pictures that do relate to a circus are the popcorn (may be eaten at a circus) and the unicycle (a circus performer may ride one).*

Elephant Cards

See pages 172–174 for ways to use the cards.

Everything Themes • ©The Mailbox® Books • TEC61260

My Circus Job

If I could be a circus performer, I would be

_____

because _____

_____.

by _____

Class Book Page: Have a child write or dictate a response to the prompt. Then have him illustrate his work. Publish the pages in a class book titled "If We Joined the Circus."

39

Name _____

Listen and Do

Draw.

40

Note to the teacher: Provide oral directions, such as "Color the animal that is dancing" or "Circle a food that comes in shells." Then specify what you would like the child to draw in the empty box by saying, for example, "Draw your favorite circus animal."

Under the Big Top

Connect the dots in order from 1 to 10.

10 •

1 •

2 •

3 •

7 •

6 •

9 •

8 •

5 •

4 •

A Jolly Juggler

Color by the code.

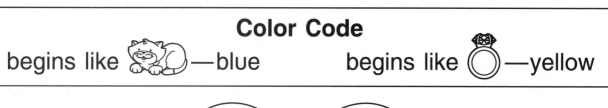

Color Code

begins like 🐱—blue   begins like 💍—yellow

Everything Themes • ©The Mailbox® Books • TEC61260

Cruising to the Circus

Color the numbers in order from 1 to 10 to make a path.

1	2	6
8	3	9

10	6	5	4	7
3	7	11	8	10
5	8	12		
7	9	10		

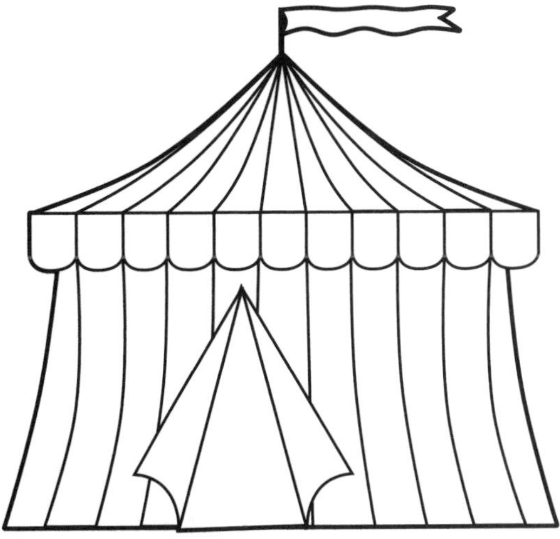

Quick Craft

Bunches of Balloons

Materials: sheet of construction paper, different colors of ink pads, crayons, scissors, glue, black marker

Directions: Color and cut out the clown. Then glue it near the bottom of the paper. Use the black marker to draw several lines (balloon strings) up from the clown's hands. At the top of each string, make a fingerprint balloon.

TEC61260

Everything Themes • ©The Mailbox® Books • TEC61260

Community Helpers

ABC

POLICE

Everything Themes • ©The Mailbox® Books • TEC61260

Note to the teacher: Read aloud the theme title. Then name each picture and invite youngsters to describe how it does or does not relate to community helpers. Have a child circle each picture that shows a community helper or something that relates to a community helper and cross out each picture that does not. *The butterfly does not relate to community helpers. Less obvious pictures that do relate to community helpers are the badge and whistle (police officers use these items) and the hard hat and hammer (a construction worker uses these items).*

45

Badge Cards

See pages 172–174 for ways to use the cards.

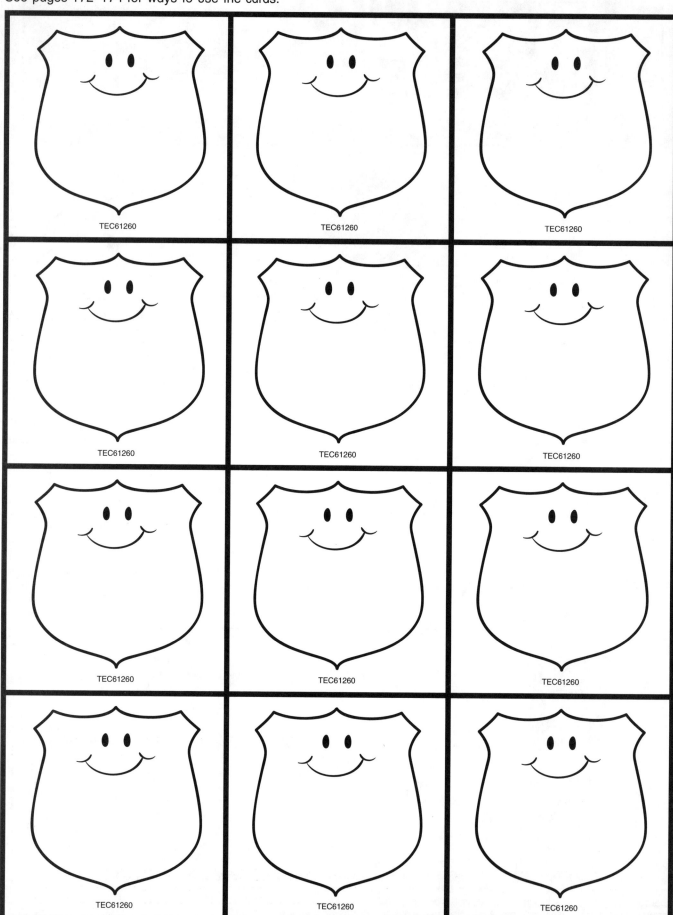

TEC61260

TEC61260

TEC61260

TEC61260

TEC61260

TEC61260

TEC61260

TEC61260

TEC61260

TEC61260

TEC61260

TEC61260

How I Would Help

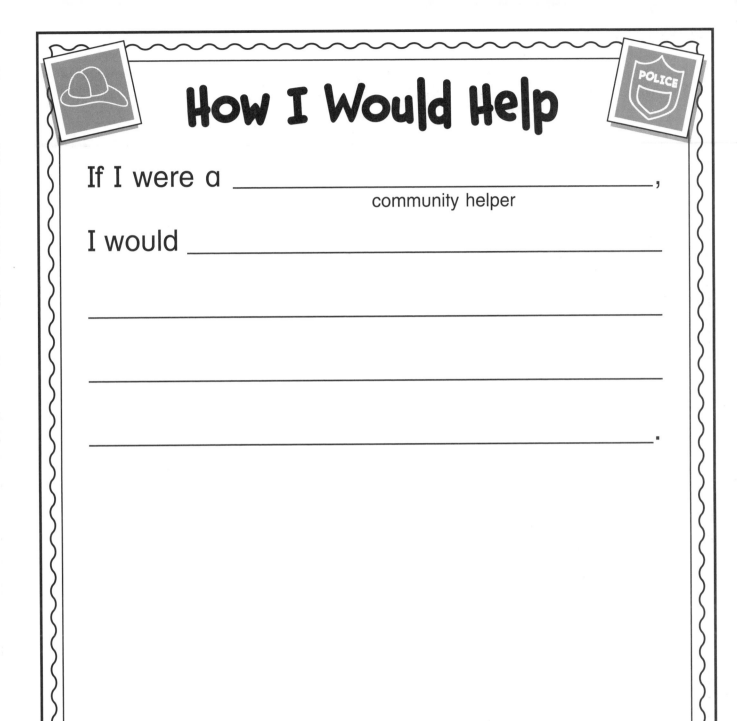

If I were a _____,
_____ community helper _____

I would _____

_____

_____

_____.

by _____

Class Book Page: Invite a child to choose a community helper and write or dictate to complete the sentence. Then have her illustrate her work. Publish the pages in a class book titled "All Kinds of Community Helpers."

Name _____

Listen and Do

Draw.

Everything Themes • ©The Mailbox® Books • TEC61260

Note to the teacher: Provide oral directions, such as "Color an item that a store clerk might use" or "Circle a hat a chef might wear." Then
specify what you would like the child to draw in the empty box by saying, for example, "Draw an item that a teacher might use."

48

A Hard Hat

Connect the dots in order from 1 to 10.

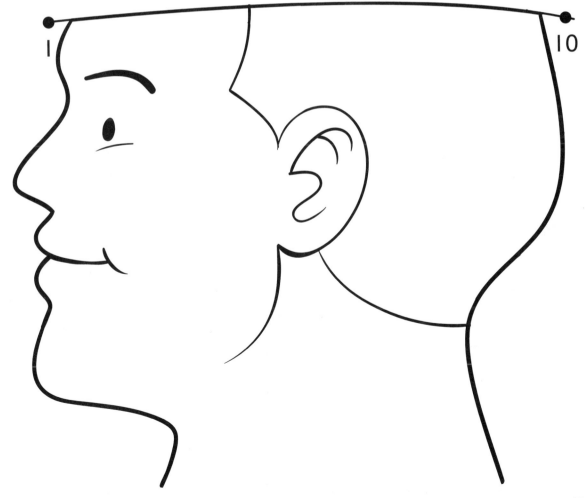

Name _____

A Big Wind

 Color a ⬚ for each word part.

Everything Themes • ©The Mailbox® Books • TEC61260

Shiny Teeth

 Cut.

Glue to match the sets.

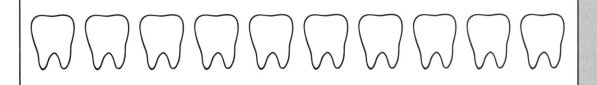

| 5 | 7 | 4 | 10 | 8 |

Quick Craft

Doctor's Bag

Materials: 9" x 12" sheet of black construction paper, 3" x 4" black construction paper rectangle, craft stick, cotton ball, crayons, scissors, glue

Directions: To make a doctor's bag, fold the sheet of construction paper in half. Then cut a handle from the paper rectangle and glue it to the bag. Color and cut out the patterns. Glue the patterns, the craft stick, and the cotton ball inside the bag.

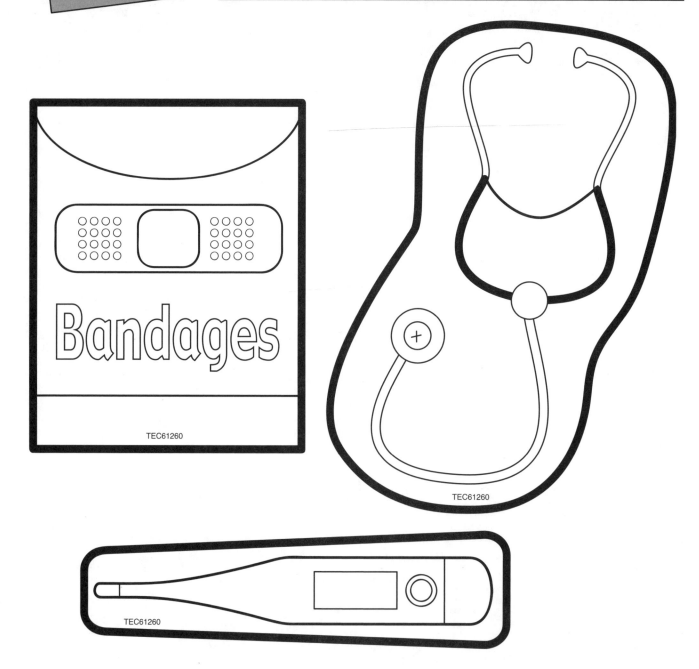

Bandages

TEC61260

TEC61260

TEC61260

Construction

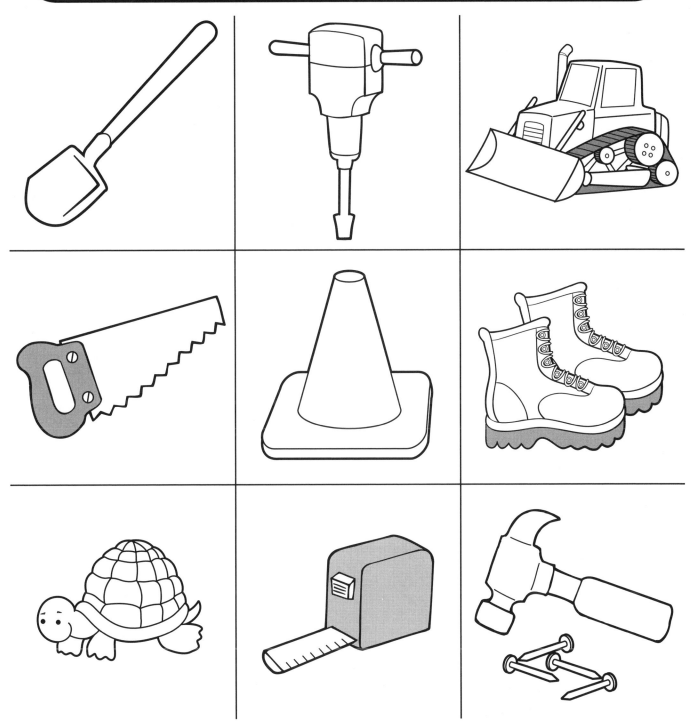

Note to the teacher: Read aloud the theme title. Then name each picture and invite youngsters to describe how it does or does not relate to construction. Have a child circle each picture that can be related to construction and cross out each picture that cannot. *The turtle does not relate to construction. Less obvious pictures that do relate to construction are the work boots (often worn by construction workers) and the shovel (some construction workers use one).*

53

Hard Hat Cards

See pages 172–174 for ways to use the cards.

TEC61260

TEC61260

TEC61260

TEC61260

TEC61260

TEC61260

TEC61260

TEC61260

TEC61260

TEC61260

TEC61260

TEC61260

Hard at Work

A construction worker can...

by _____

Class Book Page: Have a child write or dictate a response to the prompt. Then have him illustrate his work. Publish the pages in a class book titled "All About Construction Workers."

55

Listen and Do

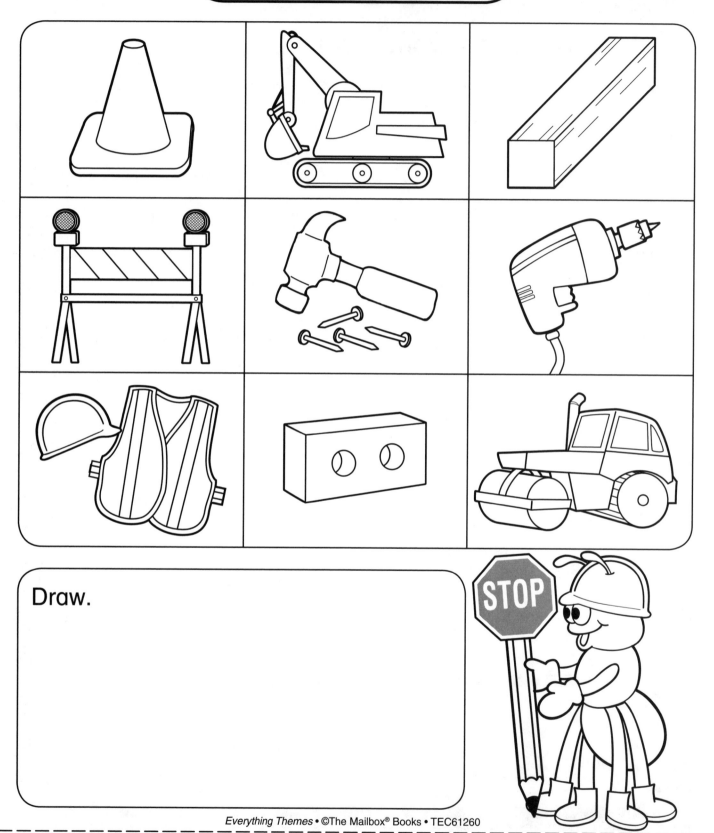

Draw.

Everything Themes • ©The Mailbox® Books • TEC61260

Note to the teacher: Provide oral directions, such as "Color the items construction workers wear for safety" or "Circle the item used to lift heavy things at a construction site." Then specify what you would like the child to draw in the empty box by saying, for example, "Draw a construction worker."

Name _____

Brick by Brick

Tear.

Glue.

Everything Themes • ©The Mailbox® Books • TEC61260

Note to the teacher: A child tears red construction paper scraps into small rectangles and glues them to the wall so they look like bricks.

57

Name _____

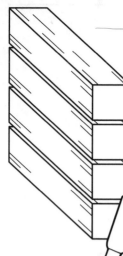

Building a House

✂ Cut.

🫙 Glue the pictures in order.

1	2	3

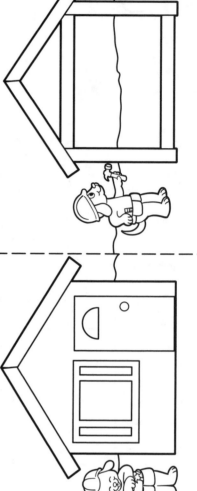

Everything Themes • ©The Mailbox® Books • TEC61260

Name _____

Work Zone

🖍 Color by the code.

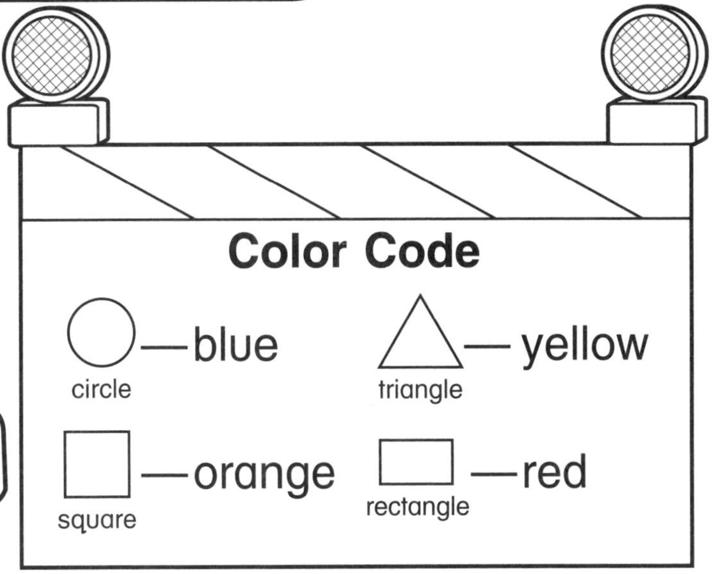

Color Code

○ —blue
circle

△ —yellow
triangle

□ —orange
square

▭ —red
rectangle

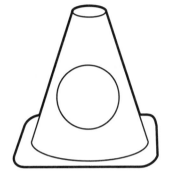
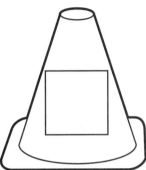
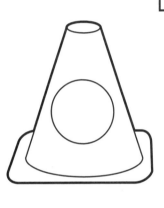

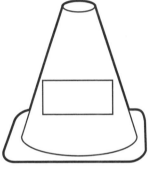
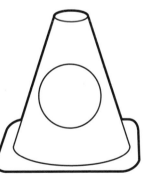

Quick Craft

A Tool of the Trade

Materials: white tagboard copy of the pattern below, 8" square of aluminum foil, crayons, scissors

Directions: Color the saw handle. Then ask for help to cut out the center of the saw handle. Place the foil atop the saw blade. Tear and fold the edges of the foil until the entire blade is covered with foil.

TEC61260

Everything Themes • ©The Mailbox® Books • TEC61260

Dinosaurs

Everything Themes • ©The Mailbox® Books • TEC61260

Note to the teacher: Read aloud the theme title. Then name each picture and invite youngsters to describe how it does or does not relate to dinosaurs. Have a child circle each picture that can be related to dinosaurs and cross out each picture that cannot. *The bike and the cat do not relate to dinosaurs. Less obvious pictures that do relate to dinosaurs are the tree (some dinosaurs ate leaves) and the nest with the eggs (dinosaurs laid eggs).*

61

Dinosaur Cards

See pages 172–174 for ways to use the cards.

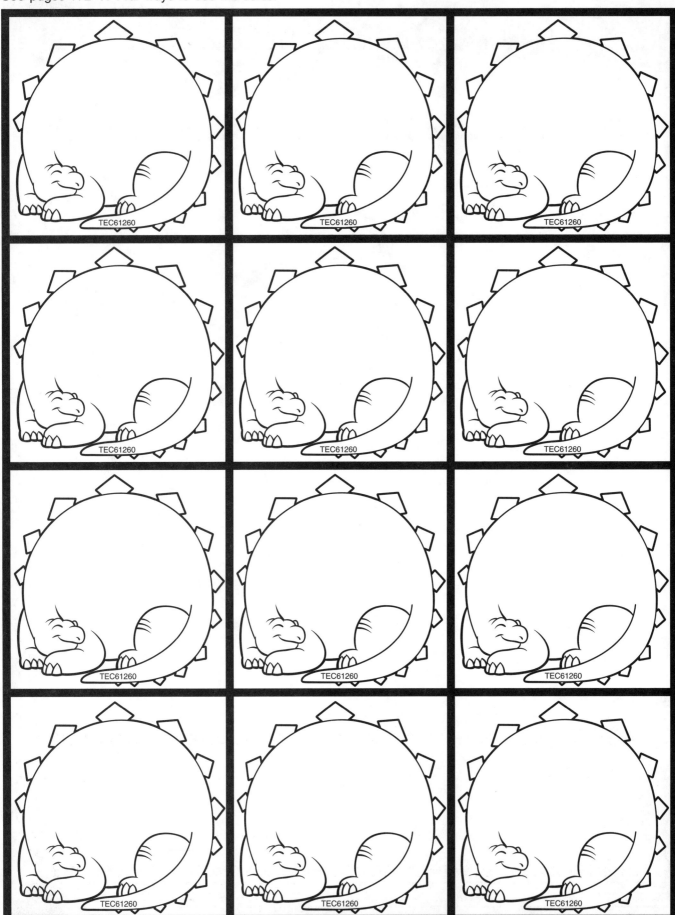

All About Dinosaurs

I know that dinosaurs…

by _____

Everything Themes • ©The Mailbox® Books • TEC61260

Class Book Page: Have a child write or dictate a response to the prompt. Then have her illustrate her work. Publish the pages in a class book titled "We Know About Dinosaurs."

Listen and Do

Draw.

Note to the teacher: Provide oral directions, such as "Cross off the *Brontosaurus*" or "Circle the nest with four eggs." Then specify what you would like the child to draw in the empty box by saying, for example, "Draw your favorite dinosaur."

Name _____

Munch, Munch, Munch!

Color.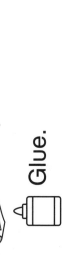

Crumple.

Glue.

Everything Themes • ©The Mailbox® Books • TEC61260

Note to the teacher: After coloring the picture, a child crumples small squares of green tissue paper and glues them to the tree so they look like leaves.

66

Keeping Watch

Color the pictures that begin like .

Everything Themes • ©The Mailbox® Books • TEC61260

Small, Medium, and Large

✂ Cut.

🍶 Glue the dinosaurs from smallest to largest.

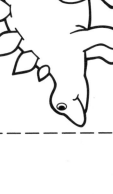

Everything Themes • ©The Mailbox® Books • TEC61260

Quick Craft

Just Hatched

Materials: white construction paper copy of this page, crayons, scissors, glue, brad fastener

Directions: Color the baby dinosaur. Cut out the patterns and cut the egg apart. Glue the baby dinosaur to the bottom half of the egg as shown. Place the top half of the egg atop the bottom half, slightly overlapping the two pieces. Use the brad to attach the egg halves.

TEC61260

TEC61260

Farm

Note to the teacher: Read aloud the theme title. Then name each picture and invite youngsters to describe how it does or does not relate to a farm. Have a child circle each picture that can be related to a farm and cross out each picture that cannot. *The octopus and the beach ball do not relate to a farm. Less obvious pictures that do relate to a farm are the overalls (may be worn by a farmer) and the glass of milk (could come from a cow on a farm).*

Sheep Cards

See pages 172–174 for ways to use the cards.

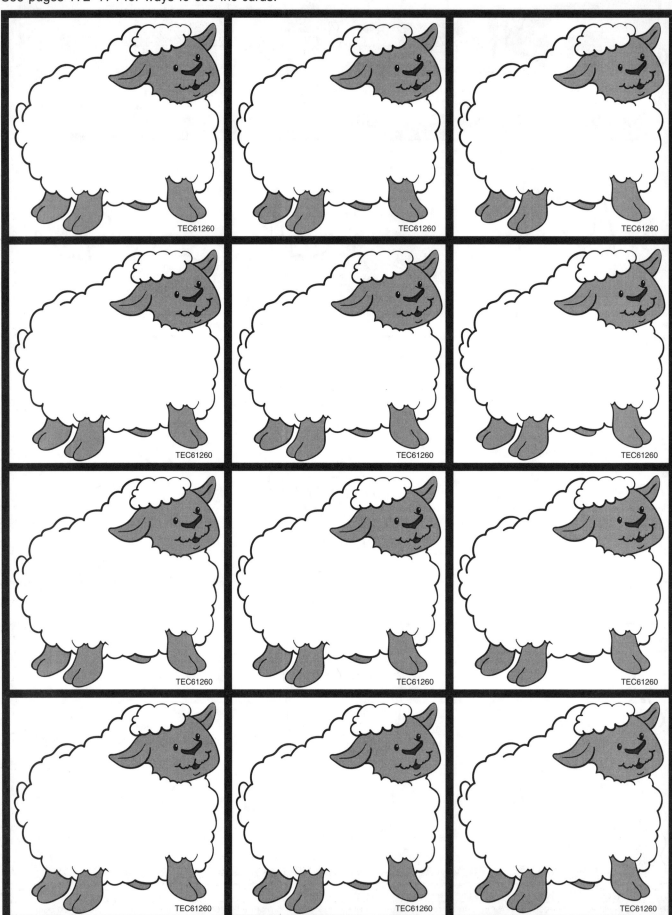

Everything Themes • ©The Mailbox® Books • TEC61260

Animals on the Farm

My favorite farm animal is

by _____

Class Book Page: Have a child write or dictate a response to the prompt. Then have him illustrate his work. Publish the pages in a class book titled "Our Favorite Farm Animals."

Listen and Do

Draw.

Note to the teacher: Provide oral directions, such as "Color the animal that quacks" or "Circle the items that could be used to milk a cow."
Then specify what you would like the child to draw in the empty box by saying, for example, "Draw a food that is grown on a farm."

A Big Barn

Trace.

A Hungry Pig

 Cut.

Glue the pictures that begin like .

Collecting Eggs

Count.

Write how many.

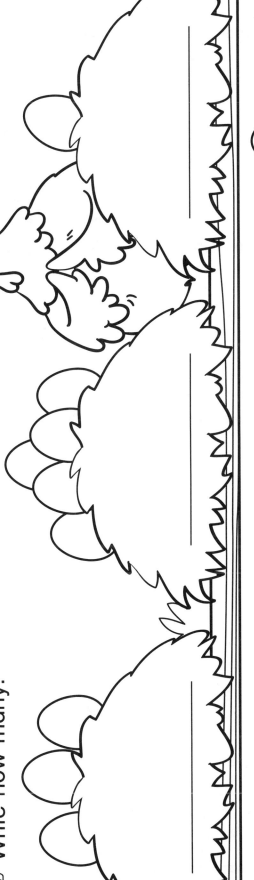

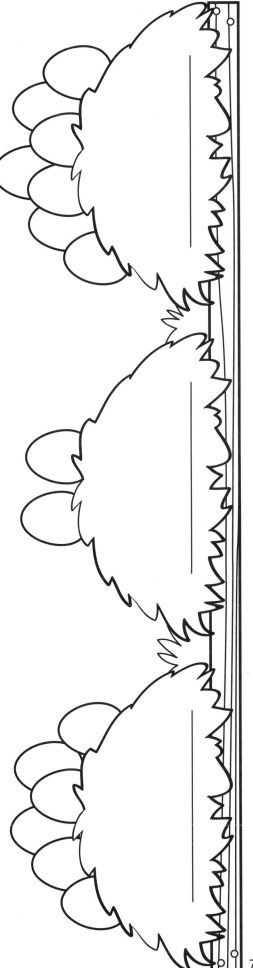

Everything Themes • ©The Mailbox® Books • TEC61260

Quick Craft

A Spotted Cow

Materials: 9" x 12" sheet of light blue construction paper, 2" x 9" rectangle of green construction paper, four 2" black tissue paper squares, glue, scissors

Directions: Tear the green construction paper into small pieces (grass) and glue the pieces along the bottom of the light blue paper. Cut out the cow pattern and glue it atop the grass. Crumple the tissue paper squares and glue them on the cow so they look like spots.

TEC61260

Forest Animals

Note to the teacher: Read aloud the theme title. Then name each picture and invite youngsters to describe how it does or does not relate to forest animals. Have a child circle each picture that can be related to forest animals and cross out each picture that cannot. *The mailbox does not relate to forest animals. Less obvious pictures that relate to forest animals are the tree (some forest animals live in trees) and the nuts (some forest animals eat nuts).*

Raccoon Cards

See pages 172–174 for ways to use the cards.

My Forest Friend

If I were friends with a/an

_____, we could

forest animal

_____

_____ .

by _____

Class Book Page: Have a child write or dictate a response to the prompt. Then have her illustrate her work. Publish the pages in a class book titled "Friendly Forest Critters."

79

Name_____

Listen and Do

Draw.

Note to the teacher: Provide oral directions, such as "Color the animal that flies" or "Circle the place an animal might live." Then specify what you would like the child to draw in the empty box by saying, for example, "Draw five nuts."

Name _____

A Big Bear

Draw to finish the bear.

Name

82

Gathering Acorns

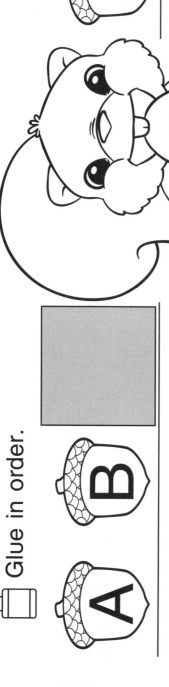

✂ Cut.
🧴 Glue in order.

J

O

N

F

H

E

Z

T

B

S

A

X

 C

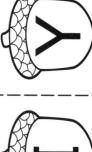 M

Y

I

R

G

Name_____

Who's in the Forest?

 Circle the matching number of animals.

2	
5	
7	
6	
10	
9	

A Sweet Bunny

Materials: paper eye, paper nose, cotton balls, brown paint, sponges, scissors, glue, marker

Directions: Sponge-paint the bunny. When the paint is dry, cut the bunny out. Glue on the eye and the nose. Then glue one or more cotton balls to the tail. Use the marker to add other details.

TEC61260

Gardening

Note to the teacher: Read aloud the theme title. Then name each picture and invite youngsters to describe how it does or does not relate to gardening. Have a child circle each picture that can be related to gardening and cross out each picture that cannot. *The ring and the whale do not relate to gardening. Less obvious pictures that do relate to gardening are the rain (it helps gardens grow) and the hat and gloves (some gardeners wear them).*

Flower Cards
See pages 172–174 for ways to use the cards.

TEC61260

TEC61260

TEC61260

TEC61260

TEC61260

TEC61260

TEC61260

TEC61260

TEC61260

TEC61260

TEC61260

TEC61260

In My Garden

If I had a garden, I would grow _____

_____

_____.

by _____

Class Book Page: Have a child write or dictate a response to the prompt. Then have him illustrate his work. Publish the pages in a class book titled "Gorgeous Gardens."

Listen and Do

Draw.

Everything Themes • ©The Mailbox® Books • TEC61260

Note to the teacher: Provide oral directions, such as "Color the item that can be used to water plants" and "Circle the items that can be used to gather vegetables." Then specify what you would like the child to draw in the empty box by saying, for example, "Draw five seeds."

Name

Tall Sunflowers

Cut.

Glue.

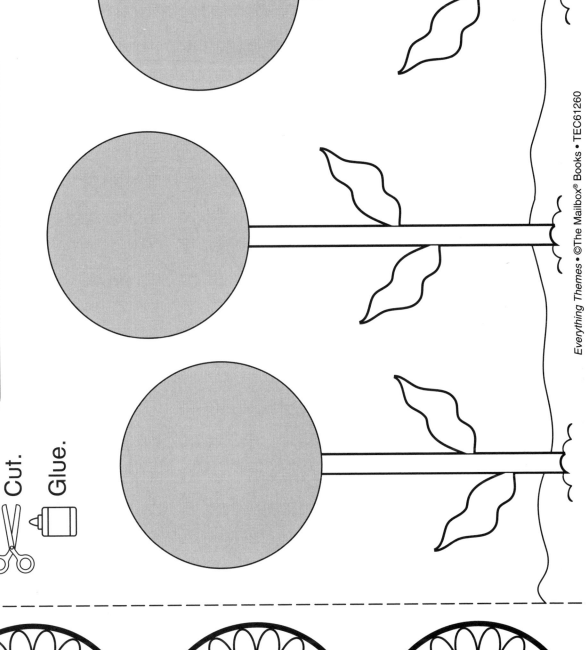

Everything Themes • ©The Mailbox® Books • TEC61260

Pretty Flowers

🖍 Color by the code.

Color Code

begins like  —yellow   begins like  —purple

begins like 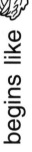 —

Giant Carrots!

 Cut.

 Glue to match one to one.

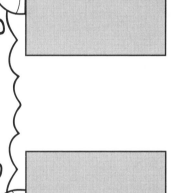 Circle.

Is there a  for each ?   :) yes   :(no

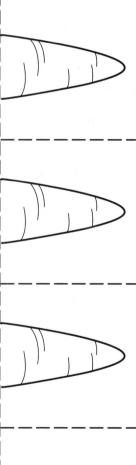

Quick Craft

Water the Garden

Materials: thin blue crepe paper streamers, sponges, paint, glue, scissors

Directions: Sponge-paint the watering can. When the paint is dry, cut out the can. Then glue streamers to the end of the spout so they look like water.

TEC61260

Ocean

Note to the teacher: Read aloud the theme title. Then name each picture and invite youngsters to describe how it does or does not relate to the ocean. Have a child circle each picture that can be related to the ocean and cross out each picture that cannot. *The banana and the nest do not relate to the ocean. Less obvious pictures that do relate to the ocean are the cruise ship (can sail on the ocean) and the island (can be found in the ocean).*

93

Fish Cards

See pages 172–174 for ways to use the cards.

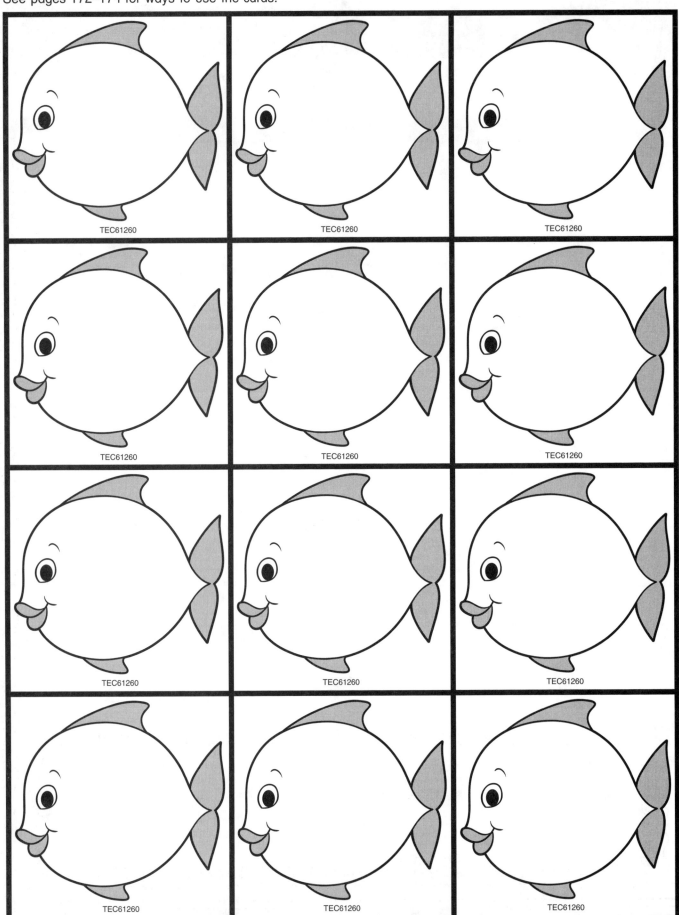

TEC61260

TEC61260

TEC61260

TEC61260

TEC61260

TEC61260

TEC61260

TEC61260

TEC61260

TEC61260

TEC61260

TEC61260

Deep Blue Sea

In the ocean you can find...

by _____

Class Book Page: Have a child write or dictate a response to the prompt. Then have her illustrate her work. Publish the pages in a class book titled "What's in the Ocean?"

Listen and Do

Draw.

Note to the teacher: Provide oral directions, such as "Color the striped fish" or "Cross out the plants that grow underwater." Then specify what you would like the child to draw in the empty box by saying, for example, "Draw an interesting seashell."

Name

Hide-and-Seek

Trace.

Underwater Friends

🖍️ Color by the code.

Color Code

begins like 🐟 —— yellow

begins like 🦀 —— red

Name_____

Under the Sea

✂️ Cut out the ⬚⬚⬚⬚⬚ .

Use the ⬚⬚⬚⬚⬚ to measure.

✏️ Write.

_____ seashells

_____ seashell

_____ seashells

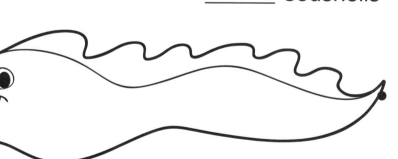

_____ seashells

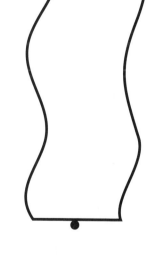

_____ seashells

Everything Themes • ©The Mailbox® Books • TEC61260

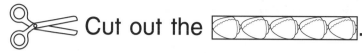

Quick Craft

Cute Crab

Materials: white construction paper copy of this page, four 12" red construction paper strips, red crayon or marker, scissors, glue

Directions: Color and cut out the crab pattern. Tear the paper strips in half. Then tear one end of each paper strip so it looks like a crab's pincers. Glue four legs to each side of the crab's body.

TEC61260

Pets

Everything Themes • ©The Mailbox® Books • TEC61260

Note to the teacher: Read aloud the theme title. Then name each picture and invite youngsters to describe how it does or does not relate to pets. Have a child circle each picture that can be related to pets and cross out each picture that cannot. *The saw and the pen do not relate to pets. Less obvious pictures that do relate to pets are the veterinarian (pets are taken to one when they are sick) and the fishbowl (certain fish might live in one).*

Doghouse Cards

See pages 172–174 for ways to use the cards.

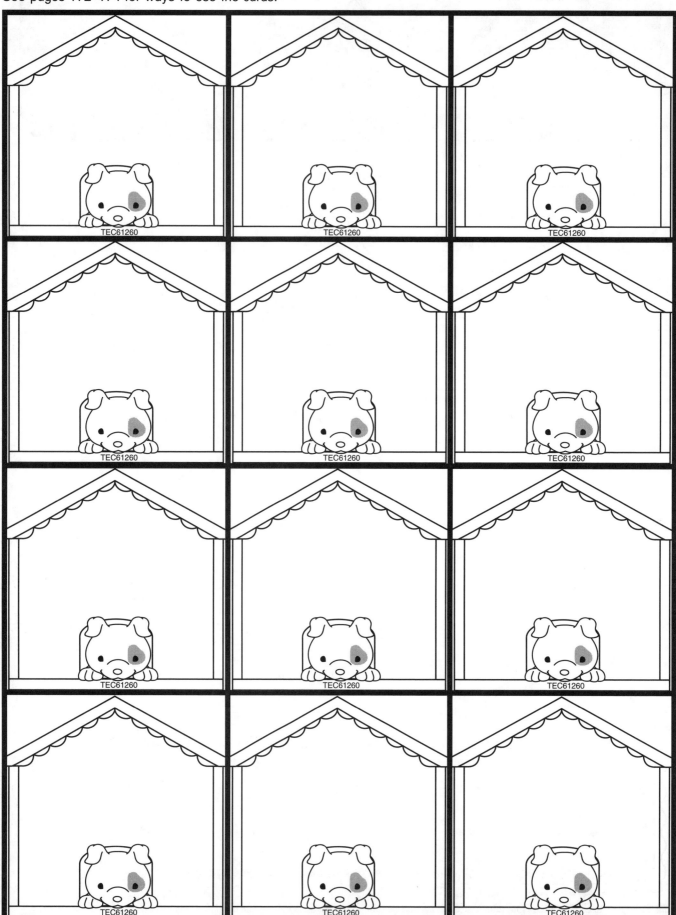

My Pet

If I could have any pet, I would want a/an

_____

because _____

_____

_____

_____.

by _____

Class Book Page: Invite a child to choose a pet. Then have her write or dictate to complete the sentence. Publish the pages in a book titled "Our Favorite Pets."

103

Listen and Do

Draw.

Note to the teacher: Provide oral directions, such as "Color the pet that barks" or "Circle the picture that shows where a hamster might live."
104   Then specify what you would like the child to draw in the empty box by saying, for example, "Draw six dog bones."

A Spotted Puppy

Color.   Tear.   Glue.

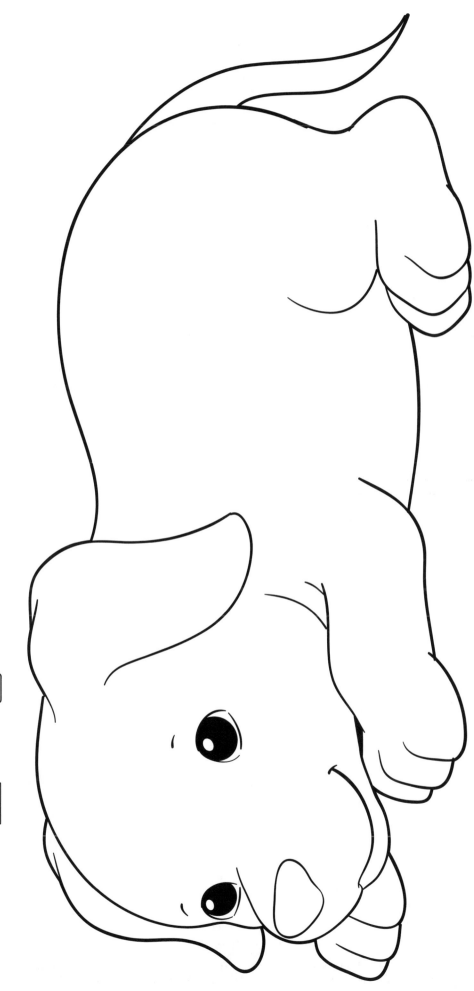

Everything Themes • ©The Mailbox® Books • TEC61260

Note to the teacher: Have a child color the puppy. Then have him tear brown and black paper scraps and glue the pieces to the puppy so they look like spots.

Name _____

106

Hamster's Home

Cut.

Glue the pictures that begin like 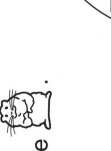 .

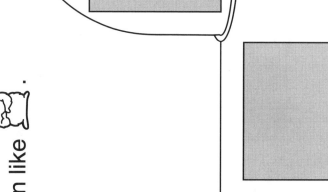

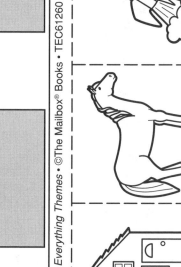

Name _____

Pet Goodies

Count.

Circle the correct number.

(8 bones)	**8** **7**
(13 yarn balls)	**11** **13**
(10 frisbees)	**10** **9**
(15 mice)	**15** **14**
(16 balls)	**16** **15**
(12 bowls)	**10** **12**

A Home for Fish

Materials: 7" paper square, construction paper scraps, blue paint, sponge, scissors, glue, crayons

Directions: Sponge-paint the fishbowl blue so it looks like water. Remove your shoe (leave your sock on) and trace your foot on the paper square. Cut out the tracing. Then use paper scraps and crayons to decorate the tracing so it looks like a fish. Glue the fish to the fishbowl and add other details to the fishbowl as desired.

TEC61260

Pond

Note to the teacher: Read aloud the theme title. Then name each picture and invite youngsters to describe how it does or does not relate to a pond. Have a child circle each picture that can be related to a pond and cross out each picture that cannot. *The computer and the lamp do not relate to a pond. Less obvious pictures that do relate to a pond are the loaf of bread (sometimes fed to ducks at a pond) and the fishing pole (people sometimes fish in a pond).*

Duck Cards
See pages 172–174 for ways to use the cards.

TEC61260

TEC61260

TEC61260

TEC61260

TEC61260

TEC61260

TEC61260

TEC61260

TEC61260

TEC61260

TEC61260

TEC61260

Everything Themes • ©The Mailbox® Books • TEC61260

What I Saw

At the pond I saw a/an _____

_____. It was

_____

_____.

by _____

Class Book Page: Have a child write or dictate to complete the sentences. Then have her illustrate her work. Publish the pages in a class book titled "Pond Sights."

Listen and Do

Draw.

Note to the teacher: Provide oral directions, such as "Color the animal with a hard shell" or "Circle the animal with feathers." Then specify what you would like the child to draw in the empty box by saying, for example, "Draw ten flies."

Name

A Fine Fish

Tear.

Glue.

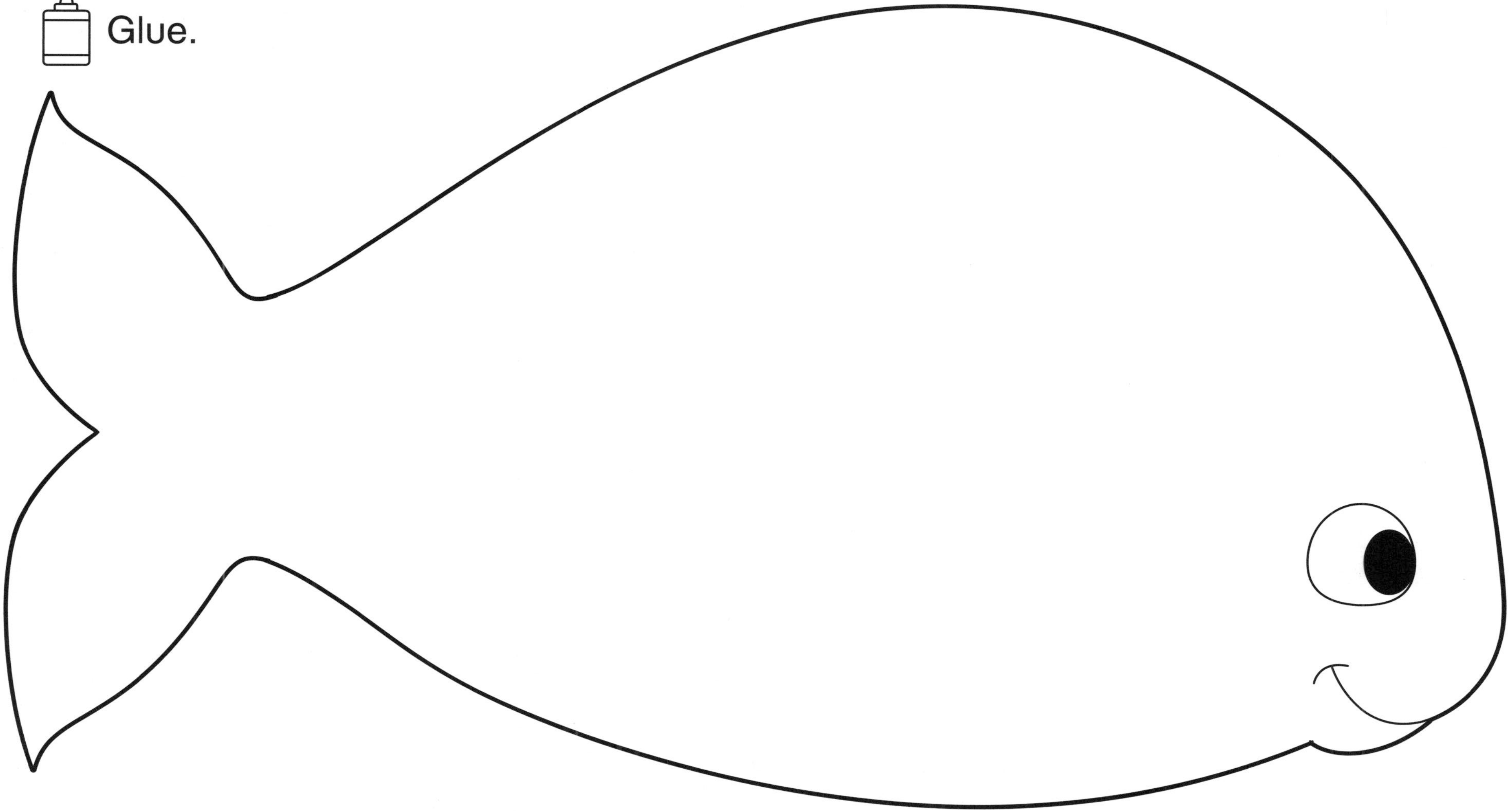

Everything Themes • ©The Mailbox® Books • TEC61260

Note to the teacher: Have each child tear construction paper scraps and glue them on the fish so they look like scales.

Name _____

Frogs on Logs

Read each uppercase letter.

Circle the matching lowercase letter.

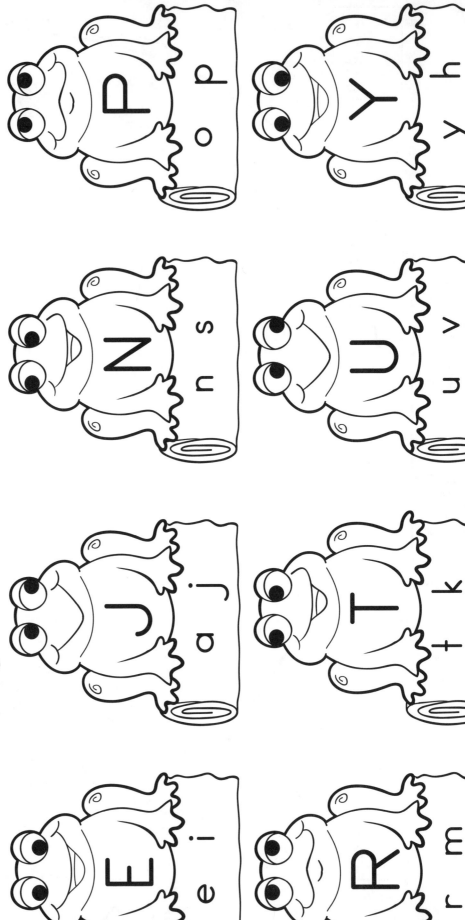

Everything Themes • ©The Mailbox® Books • TEC61260

Name

A Terrific Turtle

Color Code

less than 5—green   more than 5—brown

Color by the code.

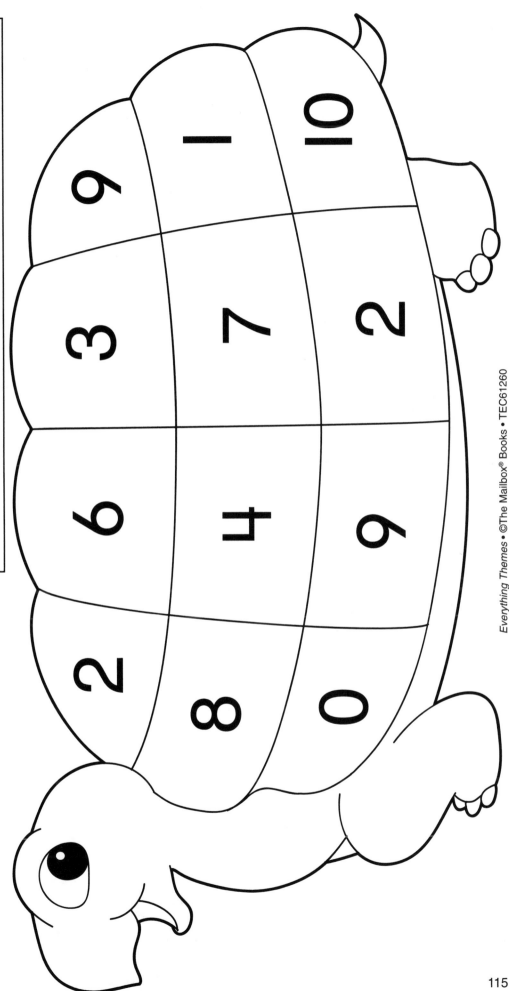

A Fly for Frog

Materials: 1" x 6" pink paper strip, sheet of white construction paper, scissors, glue, crayons

Directions: Draw a pond scene on the white paper. Then color and cut out the patterns and glue the frog to the pond scene. Accordion-fold the pink paper strip. Glue the fly to one end of the strip and then glue the opposite end of the strip to the frog's mouth where indicated.

Glue here.

TEC61260

Royalty

Note to the teacher: Read aloud the theme title. Then name each picture and invite youngsters to describe how it does or does not relate to royalty. Have a child circle each picture that can be related to royalty and cross out each picture that cannot. *The barn and the octopus do not relate to royalty. Less obvious pictures that do relate to royalty are the drawbridge (to get inside some castles, you must cross a drawbridge) and the jester (some royal families had jesters to amuse themselves).*

Crown Cards

See pages 172–174 for ways to use the cards.

TEC61260

TEC61260

TEC61260

TEC61260

TEC61260

TEC61260

TEC61260

TEC61260

TEC61260

TEC61260

TEC61260

TEC61260

For One Day

If I were king/queen for one day, I would

_____

_____

_____

_____ .

by _____

Class Book Page: Have a child circle "king" or "queen" and then write or dictate a response to the prompt. Publish the pages in a class book titled "Royal Ideas."

119

Name_____

Listen and Do

Draw.

Note to the teacher: Provide oral directions, such as "Color the castle showing the drawbridge up" or "Cross out the chair that a king normally sits in." Then specify what you would like the child to draw in the empty box by saying, for example, "Draw yourself dressed as a prince or princess."

120

Where Is It?

Draw.

Help the king find his crown.

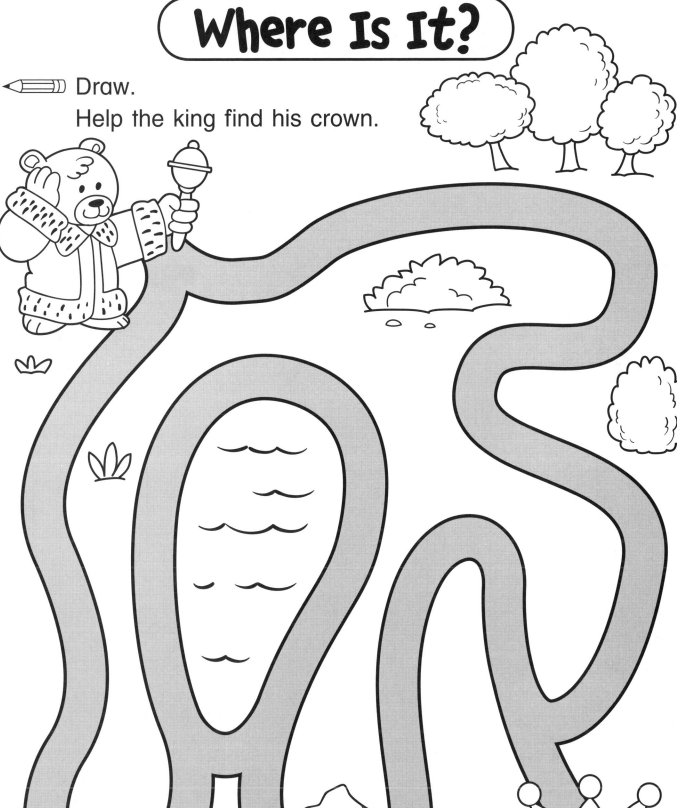

Name _____

A Gift for the King

✂ Cut.

Glue the pictures that rhyme with .

The Queen's Rings

 Count. ✏️ Write.

✏️ Circle each set that has more.

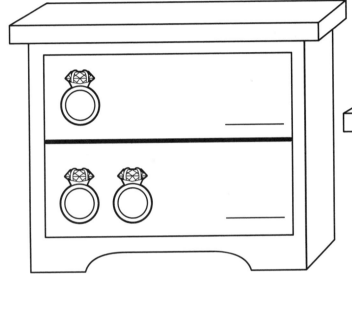

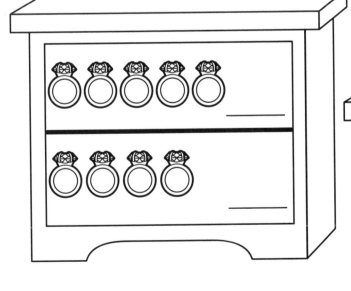

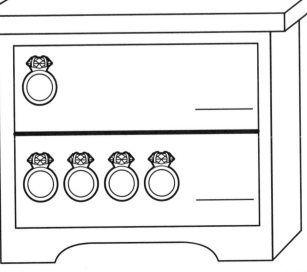

Quick Craft

Welcome to the Castle!

Materials: 8" white construction paper square, crayons, scissors, glue

Directions: Color and cut out the castle. Cut along the dotted line and fold the resulting door back. Glue the castle to the paper square, leaving the door unattached. With the door open, draw a royal person in the doorway.

Welcome!

TEC61260

Everything Themes • ©The Mailbox® Books • TEC61260

Space

Note to the teacher: Read aloud the theme title. Then name each picture and invite youngsters to describe how it does or does not relate to space. Have a child circle each picture that can be related to space and cross out each picture that cannot. *The ice cream sundae and the horse do not relate to space. Less obvious pictures that do relate to space are the shooting star (they can sometimes be seen in space) and the constellation (a group of stars seen in space).*

Star Cards

See pages 172–174 for ways to use the cards.

TEC61260

TEC61260

TEC61260

TEC61260

TEC61260

TEC61260

TEC61260

TEC61260

TEC61260

TEC61260

TEC61260

TEC61260

Space Sights!

If I took a trip in a spaceship, I might see

_____

_____

_____ .

by _____

Everything Themes • ©The Mailbox® Books • TEC61260

Class Book Page: Have a child write or dictate a response to the prompt. Then have her illustrate her work. Publish the pages in a book titled "Spaceship Trips."

Listen and Do

Draw.

Note to the teacher: Provide oral directions, such as "Color the object that astronauts use to travel to space" or "Circle the planet with rings around it." Then specify what you would like the child to draw in the empty box by saying, for example, "Draw three stars in the night sky."

128

Blast Off!

✎ Finish the spaceship.

✎ Draw your face in the window.

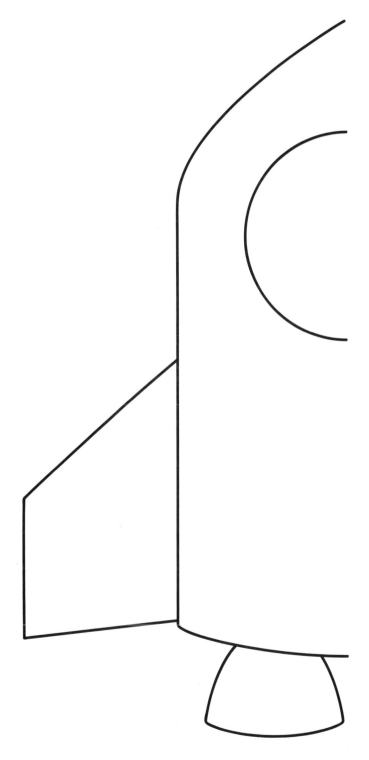

Name

Snapshots in Space

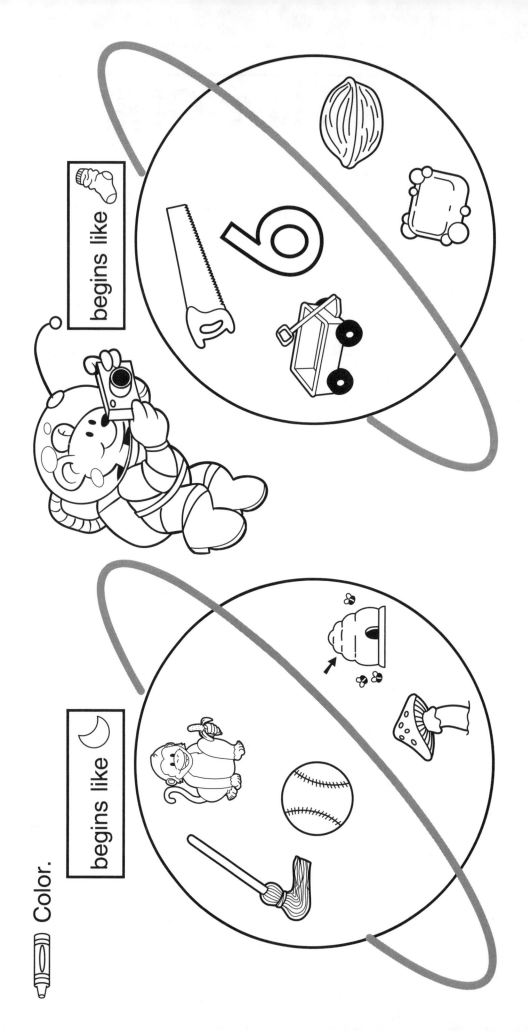

🖍 Color.

begins like 🌙

begins like 🧦

Everything Themes • ©The Mailbox® Books • TEC61260

A Starry Night

Color the matching number of stars.

3	☆ ☆ ☆ ☆ ☆ ☆ ☆ ☆ ☆ ☆
5	☆ ☆ ☆ ☆ ☆ ☆ ☆ ☆ ☆ ☆
4	☆ ☆ ☆ ☆ ☆ ☆ ☆ ☆ ☆ ☆
7	☆ ☆ ☆ ☆ ☆ ☆ ☆ ☆ ☆ ☆
9	☆ ☆ ☆ ☆ ☆ ☆ ☆ ☆ ☆ ☆
8	☆ ☆ ☆ ☆ ☆ ☆ ☆ ☆ ☆ ☆
6	☆ ☆ ☆ ☆ ☆ ☆ ☆ ☆ ☆ ☆
10	☆ ☆ ☆ ☆ ☆ ☆ ☆ ☆ ☆ ☆

A Stellar Flight

Materials: 9" x 12" sheet of black construction paper, spray bottle of diluted white paint, scissors, glue, crayons

Directions: To make a night sky, spray white paint on the black paper and set it aside to dry. Draw yourself looking out the rocket ship's window. Then color the rest of the rocket ship and cut it out. When the paint is dry, glue the rocket ship to the paper.

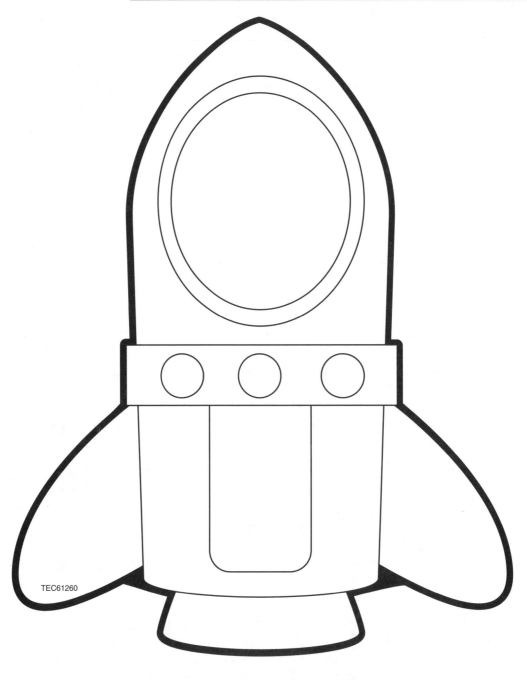

TEC61260

Sports

Note to the teacher: Read aloud the theme title. Then name each picture and invite youngsters to describe how it does or does not relate to sports. Have a child circle each picture that can be related to sports and cross out each picture that cannot. *The lamp and the barn do not relate to sports. Less obvious pictures that do relate to sports are the water bottle (often used while playing sports) and sneakers (usually worn while playing sports).*

Baseball Cards

See pages 172–174 for ways to use the cards.

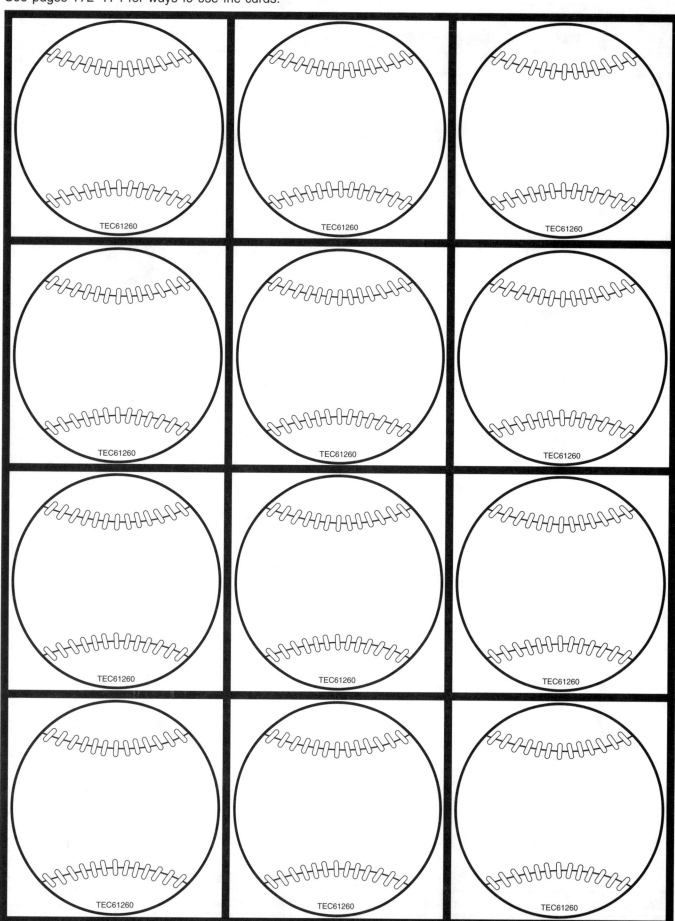

Sports Are Fun!

My favorite sport is _____

because _____

_____

_____.

by _____

Class Book Page: Have a child write or dictate to complete the sentence. Then have her illustrate her work. Publish the pages in a class book titled "Sports of All Sorts."

135

Name_____

Listen and Do

Draw.

Note to the teacher: Provide oral directions, such as "Cross out the item used to hit the ball when playing baseball" or "Circle the item you wear to protect your head when playing football." Then specify what you would like the child to draw in the empty box by saying, for example, "Draw something you use to play your favorite sport."

What a Kick!

Trace.

Name _____

Bouncing Balls

🖍 Color the pictures that begin like ⊕ orange.

What to Play?

What comes next?

 Cut.

Glue.

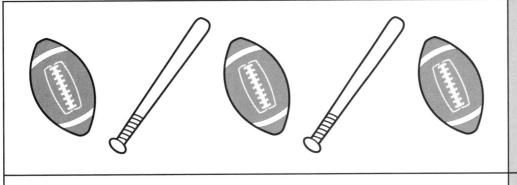

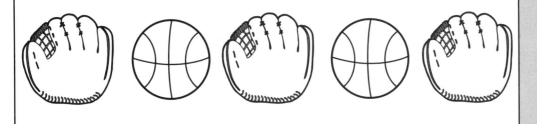

Everything Themes • ©The Mailbox® Books • TEC61260

Quick Craft

Personal Pennant

Materials: white construction paper copy of the pattern below, jumbo craft stick, crayons

Directions: Draw on the pennant an item that represents your favorite sport or team. Color and cut out the pennant; then glue a jumbo craft stick to the back to make a handle.

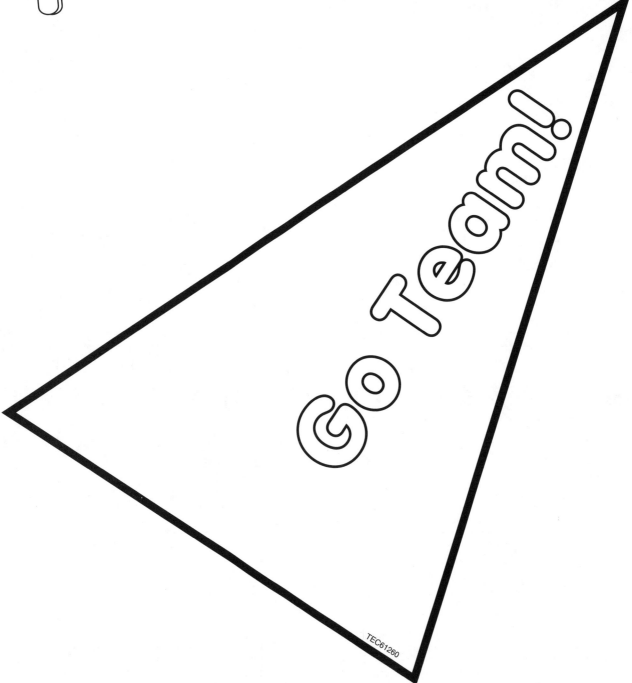

Go Team!

TEC61260

Everything Themes • ©The Mailbox® Books • TEC61260

Transportation

 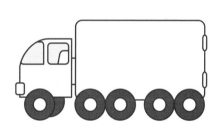 

Everything Themes • ©The Mailbox® Books • TEC61260

Note to the teacher: Read aloud the theme title. Then name each picture and invite youngsters to describe how it does or does not relate to transportation. Have a child circle each picture that can be related to transportation and cross out each picture that cannot. *The tree does not relate to transportation. Less obvious pictures that do relate to transportation are the horse (some people use them for transportation) and the sneakers (some people wear them when they walk).*

141

Bus Cards

See pages 172–174 for ways to use the cards.

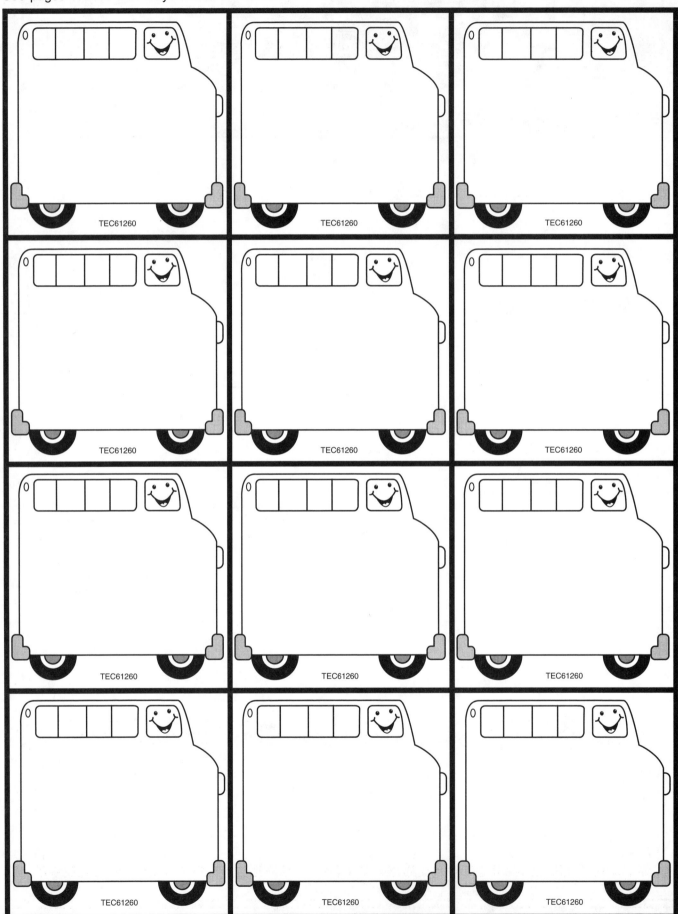

TEC61260

Everything Themes • ©The Mailbox® Books • TEC61260

Moving Along

I have ridden in/on a _____

_____.

I have not ridden in/on a _____

_____.

by _____

Class Book Page: Have a child write or dictate to complete the sentences on a copy of this page. Then have him illustrate his work. Publish the pages in a class book titled "Many Ways to Go!"

Listen and Do

Draw.

Note to the teacher: Provide oral directions such as "Color the mode of transportation with a propeller on top of it" or "Circle the item that you put in some modes of transportation to help them go." Then specify what you would like the child to draw in the empty box by saying, for example, "Draw your favorite type of transportation."

Name

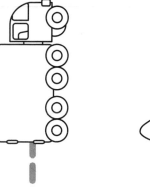

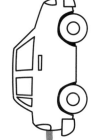
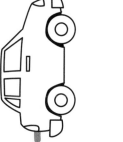
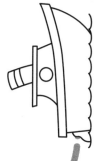

Away We Go!

Trace.

Name _____

All Aboard

 Cut.

Glue to match the ending sounds.

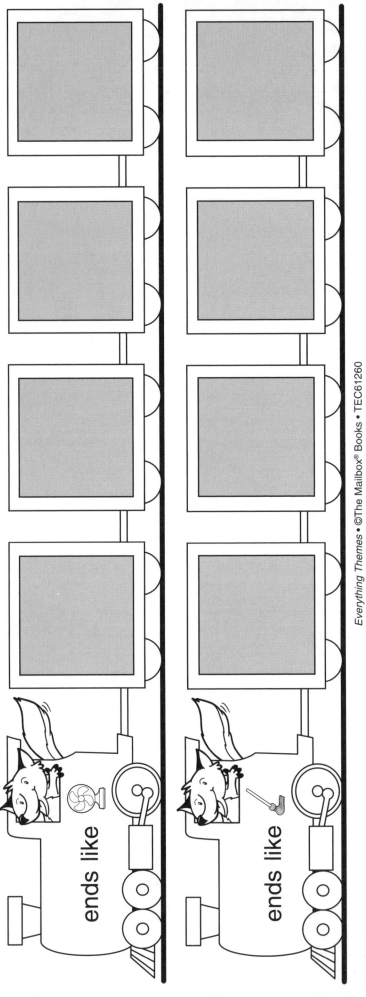

ends like

ends like

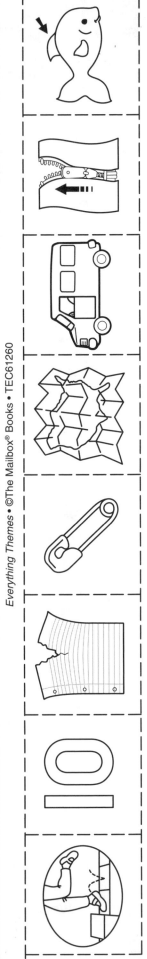

Name

High in the Sky

Color by the code.

Color Code

□—blue

○—yellow

△—orange

□—red

On Our Way

Materials: three 1½" white paper squares (windows), two 1½" black paper circles (wheels), 1" x 6" white paper strip, scissors, glue, crayons

Directions: Color and cut out the bus. Write the name of your school on the paper strip and glue it to the bus. Then glue the windows and wheels to the bus. If desired, draw a child looking out each window.

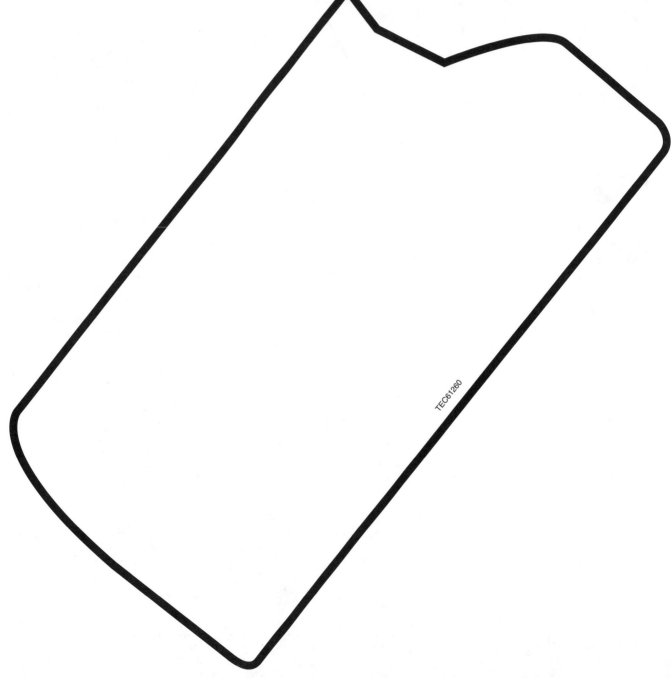

TEC61260

Everything Themes • ©The Mailbox® Books • TEC61260

Western Days

Note to the teacher: Read aloud the theme title. Then name each picture and invite youngsters to describe how it does or does not relate to western days. Have a child circle each picture that can be related to western days and cross out each picture that cannot. *The baseball items and the kite do not relate to western days. Less obvious pictures that do relate to western days are the guitar (a cowboy might play one) and the covered wagon (it was often used for travel).*

Horseshoe Cards

See pages 172–174 for ways to use the cards.

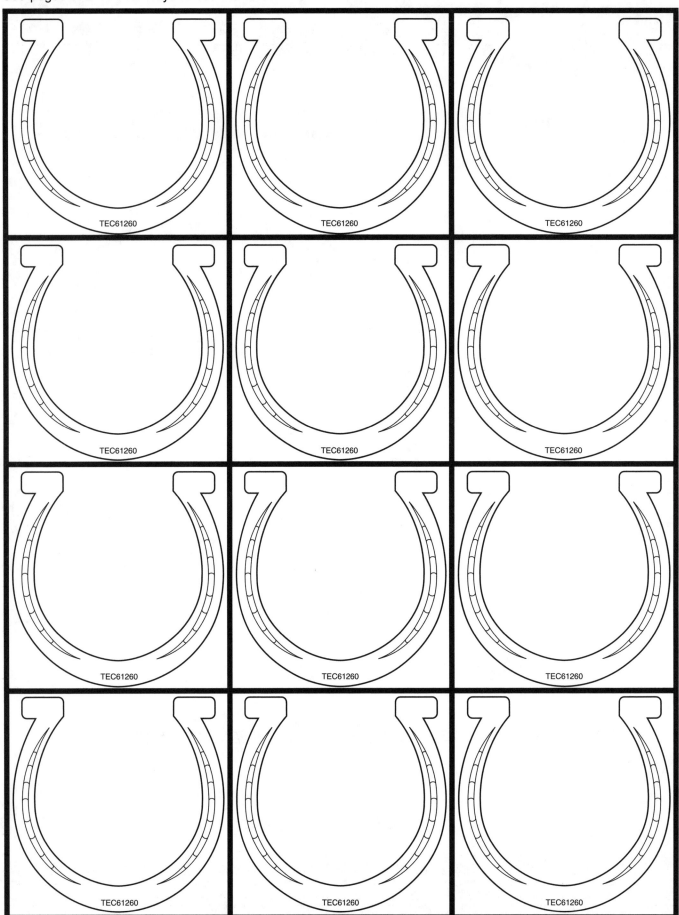

Everything Themes • ©The Mailbox® Books • TEC61260

At the Ranch

If I were a cow_____, I would _____
boy/girl

_____

_____.

by _____

Class Book Page: Have a child write or dictate a response to the prompt. Then have him illustrate his work. Publish the pages in a class book titled "Little Cowpokes."

Listen and Do

Draw.

Note to the teacher: Provide oral directions, such as "Color the animal that moos" or "Circle what a cowboy wears on his head." Then specify what you would like the child to draw in the empty box by saying, for example, "Draw the number of horseshoes a horse would wear."

Where's That Horse?

Draw.

Help the cowgirl find her horse.

Rodeo Roundup

 Cut.

Glue to match the rhyming pictures.

Everything Themes • ©The Mailbox® Books • TEC61260

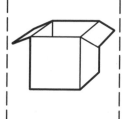     

Name

Cowboy's Closet

Draw to finish each set.

5	
7	
6	
8	

Everything Themes • ©The Mailbox® Books • TEC61260

Quick Craft

A New Hat

Materials: 7" white paper circle, 1" x 4" colored paper strip, brown paint, sponge, scissors, glue, crayons

Directions: Sponge-paint the hat pattern. When the paint is dry, cut out the hat and glue the paper strip (hatband) to it. Then draw on the circle a face that resembles your own. Glue the hat to the circle as shown.

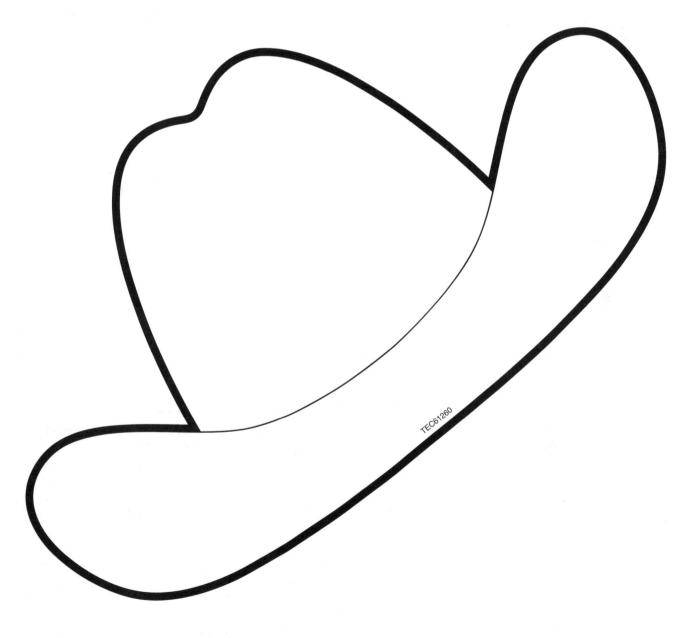

TEC61260

Zoo

Note to the teacher: Read aloud the theme title. Then name each picture and invite youngsters to describe how it does or does not relate to the zoo. Have a child circle each picture that can be related to the zoo and cross out each picture that cannot. *The piano and the dice do not relate to the zoo. Less obvious pictures that do relate to the zoo are the ice cream cone (it is sometimes eaten as a snack at the zoo) and the bench (you can sit on one to rest at the zoo).*

157

Hippo Cards
See pages 172–174 for ways to use the cards.

TEC61260

TEC61260

TEC61260

TEC61260

TEC61260

TEC61260

TEC61260

TEC61260

TEC61260

TEC61260

TEC61260

TEC61260

Everything Themes • ©The Mailbox® Books • TEC61260

My New Friend

A/An _____ followed me home
       animal

from the zoo. The _____ and I
                      animal

_____

_____

_____ .

by _____

Class Book Page: Have a child write or dictate to complete the sentences. Then have her illustrate her work. Publish the pages in a book titled "Zoo Friends."

Listen and Do

Draw.

Note to the teacher: Provide oral directions, such as "Color the animal that has black and white stripes" or "Circle the animal that has a long neck." Then specify what you would like the child to draw in the empty box by saying, for example, "Draw your favorite zoo animal."

Name

🖍 Draw.

Snazzy Stripes

Everything Themes • ©The Mailbox® Books • TEC61260

Note to the teacher: Invite each child to draw black stripes on the zebra. Encourage the youngster to experiment with different types of lines, such as straight, curvy, and zigzag.

Sleepy Cats

Cut.

Glue to match the beginning sounds.

Everything Themes • ©The Mailbox® Books • TEC61260

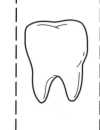

10

Hanging Out

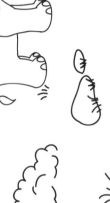

✏️ Circle.

Which has the most?

Which has the least?

✏️ Write how many.

_____

_____

Quick Craft

Lion's Hairdo

Materials: orange, yellow, and brown paper strips; paper plate; crayons; scissors; glue; unsharpened pencil

Directions: Color and cut out the lion's face. Glue the face in the center of the plate. Curl each paper strip by rolling it around the pencil. Then glue the curled strips around the rim of the plate to create the lion's mane.

TEC61260

_____
theme

On _____, our class will
    date
begin a new theme unit.

If you can donate any of the items listed below,
our class would appreciate your kindness.

- _____

- _____

- _____

- _____

- _____

If you are available to help with any of
the activities listed below, please let me
know by _____.
              date

- _____

- _____

- _____

Thanks!

Thematic Center Plans

_____ Center

_____ Center

_____ Center

_____ Center

_____ Center

_____ Center

Daily Group-Time Plans

Theme: _____   Dates: _____

Day	Whole-Group Time	Small-Group Time	Storytime
Monday			
Tuesday			
Wednesday			
Thursday			
Friday			

Field Trip Planner

Chaperones

Other Information

Destination Contact Information

Location: _____

Address: _____

Phone number: _____

Contact person: _____

Site Information

Cost: per child _____ per adult _____

Able to eat lunch on the premises? _____

Play area available? _____

Parking information: _____

**Let me tell you
what I know about**

_____.
theme

Everything Themes • ©The Mailbox® Books • TEC61260

**Let me tell you
what I know about**

_____.
theme

Everything Themes • ©The Mailbox® Books • TEC61260

**Let me tell you
what I know about**

_____.
theme

Everything Themes • ©The Mailbox® Books • TEC61260

**Let me tell you
what I know about**

_____.
theme

Everything Themes • ©The Mailbox® Books • TEC61260

Note to the teacher: Send a completed copy of a card home with each youngster to encourage him to talk with his family about the featured theme.

Theme Category Page

(See the first page of each unit.)

Whole Group: Cut apart a copy of a page and choose a theme-related card. Post the card on the board with the title shown and label two columns below it as shown. To begin, have a child name the pictured item. Then invite youngsters to brainstorm words that rhyme with the name of the pictured item. Have them identify their words as real or nonsense words as you list each word in the appropriate column on the board. Continue with other cards as desired. **Rhyming**

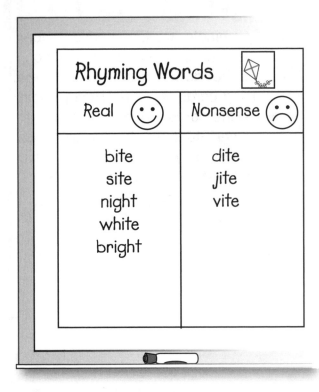

Rhyming Words	
Real 😊	Nonsense 🙁
bite	dite
site	jite
night	vite
white	
bright	

A firefighter is a community helper because he fights fires.

Whole Group: Cut apart a copy of a page and place the resulting cards in a bag. Have youngsters sit in a circle and pass the bag as you play soft music. Stop the music and direct the child holding the bag to remove a card, name the pictured item, and tell how it is or is not related to the theme. Continue until each card has been used. **Identifying items from a theme**

Everything Themes • ©The Mailbox® Books • TEC61260

Partners: Laminate two construction paper copies of a page and cut them apart, setting aside the cards that do not relate to the theme. Mix the remaining cards together. Have a pair of students use the cards to play a version of the game Go Fish! Students play the game as usual, but instead of saying "Go fish!" they say a predetermined theme-related phrase, such as "Go pick!" for the apple theme or "Go dig!" for the construction theme. **Participating in a game**

Do you have an ear of corn?

Go plow the field!

Small Group: Cut apart a copy of a page, setting aside the cards that do not relate to the theme. Place the remaining cards facedown in your group area. Have a child turn over a card and name the pictured item. Continue in this manner until each card is faceup. Then invite students to guess what the featured theme is based on the items pictured on the cards. **Critical thinking**

Small Group: To prepare, program the cards with consecutive numbers; then cut them apart. Give each child in the group a card, making sure the cards distributed have consecutive numbers. The students use the numbers on their cards to arrange themselves in numerical order from smallest to largest. After checking for accuracy, give each child a different card and repeat the activity. **Ordering numbers**

Center: Use copies of the cards to make uppercase letter cards, ensuring there are enough of each of the letters for every child to spell his name. Make a name card for each student and place the name cards and letter cards at a center. A child locates his name card. Then he finds the appropriate letters and spells his name. **Name recognition and spelling**

Center: Program three copies of the page to make a set of alphabet cards. Set aside the extra cards. Mix the cards and place them faceup on a large theme-related cutout. (For example, make a blue wave cutout for the ocean unit or a red barn cutout for the farm unit.) Also place an alphabet strip at the center. A child places each card below the corresponding letter on the alphabet strip. **Matching letters**

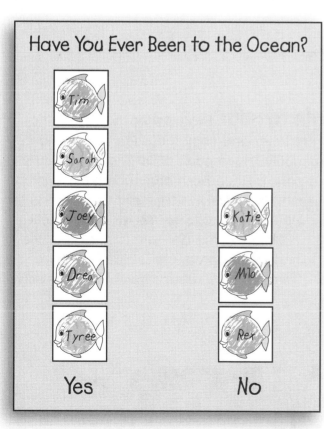

Whole Group: Cut apart a class supply of the cards. Have each child color a card; then help her personalize it. Post a graph labeled with an appropriate theme-related question and answer choices, similar to the one shown. Invite each student, in turn, to announce her answer to the question as you help her place her card in the corresponding column. After each child has positioned her card, discuss the results of the graph with the group. **Graphing**

Center: Make three different-colored copies of a page of cards and cut the cards apart. Mix the cards and place them in a container at a center along with a 12" x 18" sheet of paper (sorting mat) in each of the three colors. A child sorts each card onto the appropriate mat. **Sorting by color**

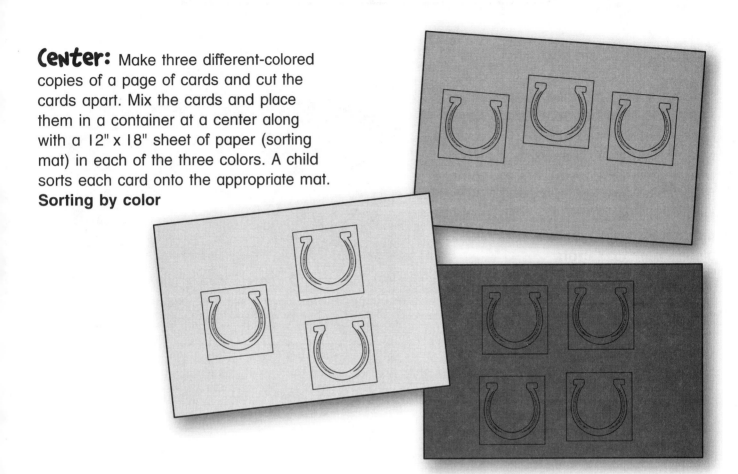

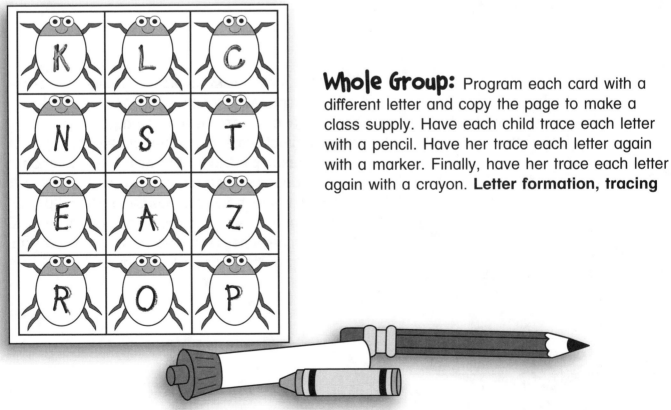

Whole Group: Program each card with a different letter and copy the page to make a class supply. Have each child trace each letter with a pencil. Have her trace each letter again with a marker. Finally, have her trace each letter again with a crayon. **Letter formation, tracing**

"Listen and Do" Page

Individual: Give each child a copy of a page, a paper strip, and a thematic cutout. Have each child glue the cutout to the center of her paper strip. Then have her color the pictures on the page and cut them out to make cards. Direct her to glue some or all of the cards to the cutout and paper strip as desired. To make a headband, fit each child's strip around her head and staple the ends in place. **Making a craft**

Center: Laminate two copies of a page and place them at a center along with a supply of dry-erase markers. For each picture on the page, have one child give directions for the other student to follow by saying, for example, "Color the nest with two eggs brown." Youngsters take turns giving and following directions until each page is complete. When students are finished, have them wipe off the pages to ready the center for the next visitors. **Giving and following oral directions**

Individual: Have each child choose four pictures on a copy of a page to color and cut out. Next, have him glue each picture to a separate 5½" x 8½" piece of paper and then write or dictate a sentence about each. When he's satisfied with his work, help him stack the pages between two 6" x 9" construction paper covers and staple them along the side. **Writing**

At the circus, you can see clowns.

Small Group: Cut apart a copy of the page to make picture cards and place two plastic hoops on the floor as shown. Lead the students in naming the items pictured. Then help the group determine a criterion by which to sort the cards. Label each hoop with a sorting criterion; then direct each child to choose a card and place it in the corresponding hoop. Continue until all of the cards have been sorted. **Sorting**

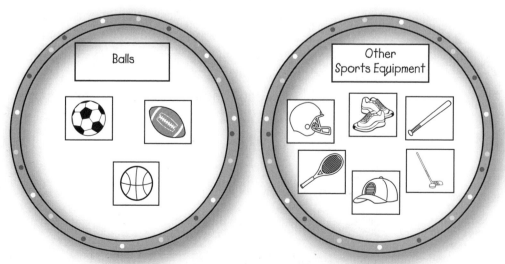

Balls

Other Sports Equipment